ALSO BY TERRY PRONE

FICTION
The Scattering of Mrs Blake
Blood Brothers, Soul Sisters
Racing the Moon
Running Before Daybreak
Dancing with the Angel
Swinging on a Star

NON-FICTION
Just a Few Words
Get That Job
Do Your Own Publicity
Be Your Own Boss
Irish Murders 1 and 2
Mirror, Mirror: Confessions of a Plastic Surgery Addict
This Business of Writing (with Kieran Lyons)
Talk the Talk
The Best Advice I Ever Got
What Every Working Woman Should Know – and Do

WRITE AND GET PAID FOR IT

TERRY PRONE

LONDUBH BOOKS

In memory of Kieran Lyons, a generous friend

First published in 1979 by Turoe Press

This revised edition published by Londubh Books 2010

Londubh Books, 18 Casimir Avenue, Harold's Cross, Dublin 6w

Part of Chapter 14, 'Writing for the Spoken Word', appeared in *Talk the Talk*

(Currach Press, 2007)

www.londubh.ie

1 3 5 4 2

Cover by Sin É design; cover image © Corbis

Origination by Londubh Books

Printed in Ireland by ColourBooks, Baldoyle Industrial Estate, Dublin 13

ISBN: 978-1907535-04-8

About the Author

Terry Prone is Chairman of the Communications Clinic in Dublin. A freelance writer, magazine editor, scriptwriter, novelist and award-winning short-story writer, she has trained journalists, broadcasters and businesspeople in all aspects of communication and is one of Ireland's most in-demand after-dinner speakers. She is married to Tom Savage, and their only son, Anton, is Managing Director of the Communications Clinic.

Acknowledgements

Each update of this book reinforces a joyful truth I discovered first time around: that writers, while in theory they're in competition with each other, are in fact generous and mutually supportive. Particularly women writers. Those who, this time around, gave time and advice were Cathy Kelly, Marian Keyes and Mary Hosty. Editors who were willing to have their brains picked include Peter Murtagh, Managing Editor of *The Irish Times*, Ger Colleran, Editor of the Irish *Star*, Sebastian Hamilton, Editor of the Irish *Mail on Sunday*, Claire Grady, Executive Editor of the *Evening Herald*. Adrian Weckler of the *Sunday Business Post* was extremely helpful, as was blogger Suzy Byrne. Gerard Kenny, my colleague at the Communications Clinic, was, as always, the ultimate human resource.

I'm grateful to Maeve Binchy, Rita Mae Brown, Liam Nolan and many others quoted in the book for their willingness, down the years, to answer questions about their trade. Above all, thanks to Jo O'Donoghue of Londubh Books, who keeps me at it.

Contents

1

So You Want to Be a Writer

If a Writer has to rob his Mother he will not hesitate;
The 'Ode on a Grecian Urn' is worth more than
any number of Old Ladies.

William Faulkner

The first edition of this book was published thirty years ago. It wasn't my idea. A publisher and friend named Catherine Rose thought it up. 'You get a lot of stuff into newspapers,' she said. 'I'd like you to write a book about how to do it.'

I couldn't get over it. I was thrilled. Until I rang my mother to boast, and met with one of those wet-blanket responses only a mother can deliver.

'That's fine,' she said.

Now you know, and I know, that when your mother says something is 'fine' or 'grand', it doesn't mean she's ecstatic about it. It means she's grimly despondent and it's your job to make her tell you why.

'You're not as enthusiastic as I expected,' I said, trying to hang on to the delight.

'It's a great honour, all right,' she said, in a measured way.

'But you don't want me to do it?'

'That's up to you.'

This was said in the tone used to advise children who want to stick their heads out of the window of a moving train that a percussive encounter with a passing lamp-post might be the consequence.

'What's the disadvantage?'

'You'll be giving away all your secrets to your competitors,' she announced. 'They'll take all your jobs and then where will you be?'

I wish I could tell you that I felled her with an evidenced argument but that wouldn't be true. She'd chilled my heart and convinced me that three weeks after the publication of *Write and Get Paid for It!* I would be begging in the street. But I knew I was going to do it anyway, seduced, as I was (and still am, if you must know) by the prospect of holding my own book in my hand.

When the book came out, it went straight to the top of the bestseller lists, which at least served to dent my mother's despondency a bit. I still got work from newspapers, radio programmes and TV shows. Now and again, another writer working for the same paper or programme would sidle up to tell me that they had got into the business as a result of reading *Write and Get Paid for It!* There seemed to be enough work to go around.

But the fascinating outcome was the stories told by individuals who wrote to me or visited me in the following months and years. Like the woman from the west of Ireland who wanted to see me but could not be persuaded to be specific about why. When she arrived, she was clutching a battered copy of the book, interleaved so much with her own notes that the spine was hanging on by a thread. She explained that, hospitalised with a complicated case of Myasthenia Gravis, she had been in despair about mounting bills and her inability to pay them, when a friend visited her and tossed the shiny new paperback on the bed, telling her that since she was going to be bedridden, she might usefully use the paperback to learn to do the one thing you can do without ever setting foot to the floor: write.

The patient started to study the little volume with a fierce concentration. Then to draft features for newspapers. Then to submit them. (Her husband acted as postman.) Sometimes they vanished and she never heard another word about them. Sometimes they were tersely rejected. But enough of them were published to allow her to earn £18,000 that first year. (This phenomenal amount of cash, thirty years ago, floored the NUJ when she applied to be a member of the freelance branch. They didn't believe her and made her prove it.) She has also published books, presented radio programmes and advised on TV programmes.

Another reader's father arrived into the hospital where she was being treated, told her he had always thought she had the makings of a writer and that maybe this would give her a kick start. She's since had ten or eleven international bestsellers.

What the book did for countless readers was to remove some of the fear and most of the excuses that prevent talented people from ending up in print.

The fear is that any form of publication is an abstruse, closed-off entity like a medieval fortress, repelling all would-be boarders by barrier systems the occupants refuse to share with anybody. The reality is that boarders often learn about the systems, refuse to follow them and then get good and mad because they don't meet with acceptance. Which is a little like a soldier complaining that the lads in the fort wouldn't let him in, even though he never knocked on the front door or gave the password.

Be clear. This book will give you an understanding of how editors on newspapers and in publishing houses, as well as literary agents, view new work, how best to present it to them and what pitfalls to avoid. But the biggest single obstacle for you, if you passionately want to be a published writer, is the deadly internal voice that puts a million negative possibilities into your mind whenever the dream floats through it. These negative possibilities turn first into predictions and then into excuses, letting you off the hook of attempting what the deadly voice suggests is a waste of time anyway.

Here are just some of the discouraging possibilities the deadly negative voice whispers:

You Might Get a Rejection Slip

If you're lucky, you'll get a rejection slip. These days, people in publishing are so pressured that they tend to use silence as the clearest form of rejection. If you haven't heard from them, you can figure your oeuvre hasn't rendered them orgasmic. But if, when you get an electronic rejection slip or meet with complete silence, you decide that this ends your career and leaves you only with the option of shoving your manuscript in a desk drawer and locking it, you're missing the chance to join an impressive line-up of writers who, at the outset, were rejected in the most humiliating terms.

John D. MacDonald, the American thriller writer (*One Fearful Yellow Eye* and *Condominium*) produced 800,000 unsaleable words before his stories began to be picked up by the pulp magazines of the day. Within ten years, his name on the cover of a book automatically gave it bestseller status.

Richard Bach, the author of one of the biggest bestsellers of the twentieth century, *Jonathan Livingston Seagull*, had the manuscript rejected by sixteen publishers – and then accepted by one who had earlier rejected it. More than a hundred publishers failed to see any merit in *Zen and the Art of Motorcycle Maintenance*. J.P. Donleavy had *The Ginger Man* turned down by thirty publishers. He went on to own the company that first accepted it.

Rejection doesn't confine itself to living writers. An American author, maddened by having his work turned down, typed into his computer the first chapter of a William Faulkner novel, added an outline of the book and sent it off to twelve publishers. Seven refused it immediately and – even more worryingly – only three out of the twelve spotted it for what it was.

The point is that with practice, determination, a modicum of talent and some attention to the marketplace, the flow of negative responses tends to diminish and become balanced by the flow of cheques. Paying attention to the marketplace means realising that, for example, the market for *noir* novels about the worst years of the Troubles in Northern Ireland is somewhat thin and also that if you send something to the *Pig Breeders' Weekly* more suited to *Lingerie Newsletter*, the pig people may not bother to go to the trouble of a formal negative response.

Always remember that a rejection does not disqualify you as a writer for ever. All it means is that one particular editor of one particular publication on one particular day did not think one particular piece you sent suited the needs of their magazine.

Nor should you believe that having your work turned down is a rite of passage only – that it happens in the early days but, once you are recognised as a professional writer, ceases forever. It doesn't. Sean O'Casey got a rejection from *Playboy* in his later years. His widow told me it deeply depressed him. Fame and an assured place in the literary establishment not only failed to insulate him against the pain of rejection but arguably made him more sensitive to it.

Having a reputation and a standing neither preserves you from rejection nor comforts you when it happens. When someone tells you your work isn't acceptable to them you feel much worse, if you've been thirty years at the writer's keyboard, than you felt when you were a beginner. You feel shamed, found-out, humiliated, dated and reduced to a pile of steaming poo. You damn the publisher, editor or producer to hell in your own mind. But you quickly start working on how to fix the manuscript so that it will appeal to someone else. Because, when you're a long time on the go as a writer, you learn resilience.

Next time you get a rejection, apply Prone's Law of the Rejection Slip to it. That law holds that refusals never come except when you are depressed and poor and then they come in sheaves. But no editor sending you a rejection message knows that any other editor has sent you one, and the fact that several do so at the same time should be taken a) as a painful coincidence and b) as a cue for you to dust yourself off and start again.

You Think You're Too Old or Too Young
Impossible. At the younger end of things, the earlier you start the better. You can perfect your craft long before you leave

school and build up a useful portfolio of published work. Remember, when you submit by email, the recipient doesn't know what you look like so they can't work out whether you're thirteen or thirty-two. If your piece is well written, they'll be interested and your revealing your extreme youth at that point will be an advantage, rather than a disadvantage.

There is no upper age-limit, either. Provided you don't get bogged down in an archaic style awash in clues to your age ('frock' for 'dress', 'blouse' for 'shirt' or 'top' or references to the smell of mothballs), no editor will know whether you're sixteen or sixty. My father wrote funny pieces for magazines in his early twenties before becoming distracted by a full-time job and a family. When he retired, we gave him a little Brother portable typewriter. Within a few months, he had submitted a few features (sensibly concentrating on retirement magazines) and improved his happiness level and finances at one and the same time. The gap of forty years didn't show up in his work, which was as energetic and amusing as it had been in his early days.

Occasionally, someone publishes sporadically. Let's say a short story a year. These make no particular impact. Then the writer suddenly springs to fame at an advanced age. The classic case is E. Annie Proulx (the L and the X are silent) whose first novel, *Postcards*, was published when she was in her mid-fifties. It won prestigious literary awards. It was speedily followed by *The Shipping News*, which won just about every literary award available.

In short, to misquote a singing seventy-year-old: what's age got to do with it?

You Were Not the Best Student in English in Your Class at
School or Found Studying English at Third Level Tough Going
So? If you want to be a freelance journalist, the capacity to
write the sort of filigreed English your schoolteacher might
have loved is irrelevant. Similarly, if you want to write a novel,
knowing all about deconstructionism is going to be of damn
all use to you. The education system is a process to be survived
and surmounted. Ideally with lots of extra-curricular reading.

If you read a lot, can write clear understandable English,
tell a story or argue a point, your school or college marks
are beside the point. And if you cannot do all four, it doesn't
matter how good or bad you were at classroom work. If you
have not read a book since you were forced to in university
or school, *that* is a problem. If you never read newspapers
but spend your time Twittering and texting and looking up
the celeb section of breaking news sites, that's a much greater
disadvantage than having been a literary also-ran in sixth
class.

Writers, from Julius Caesar to the present day, have usually
been addicted to reading. Charles Lamb said that whenever he
wasn't walking, he was reading. Dr Johnson was short-sighted
enough to qualify, these days, for disability allowances. He
nonetheless held a book millimetres away from his eyes as he
walked, 'stepping over shadows and stumbling over sticks and
stones'. Oscar Wilde, as a child hooked on books, imagined
himself as the hero of every one of them, because, as he put it,
'the life of books had begun to interest me more than real life'.

More recently, Galway thriller writer Ken Bruen stumbled
his way through childhood because he, too, was never
far from a book. 'I committed a cardinal sin as a kid,' the
Guardian quotes him as admitting. 'I never spoke, and my

mother thought there was something seriously wrong with me. A silent child is regarded as a problem in Ireland and I just read all the time.' By so doing, he was qualifying himself for his later career as a writer.

It's odd. Nobody in their right minds would assume that they could breed the winner of the Derby without being steeped in horses from birth, just as nobody would think they could create a great garden without visiting other people's gardens and watching experts on TV. Yet some people who have never read a book believe – wrongly – that they can easily become writers. They have about as much chance as someone with a tin ear and no habit of listening to music has of leading the RTÉ Symphony Orchestra.

You Want an Enormous Advance and a Weekly Newspaper Column

Ah, now. Ah, please. Get a grip. Yes, of course, it has happened that a brand-new novel has won itself a vast advance. But if you want to play those kind of odds, you're better investing in a Monday Millions ticket with the National Lottery. Ditto with getting a newspaper column. Most writers, despite the constant attention given to the high-flying exceptions, spend a long time at their craft before becoming an overnight success. In addition, you have to think of the times that are in it. Which are bad. Worldwide.

The times are bad not only for the property market. They're particularly bad for those who earn their living by the printed word. Newspapers are in trouble everywhere, and most of the familiar names in publishing are now owned by massive multinational corporations which demand that they make a profit. Every year. Every quarter. Editors at these publishing houses have less and less discretion. As recently as five years ago, for instance, sums of up to a quarter of a million Euro were being lashed at Irish celebrities for tell-all autobiographies. It's not happening any more, for two reasons. First of all, the ones who were expected to tell all either had damn all to tell or damn all that we hadn't read already somewhere else. Secondly, the available pot of dosh for new writers was reduced by the international economic downturn and the fact that some of the earlier tell-all books had turned out to be lemons.

Of course, smaller, boutique publishers may take a punt on an unknown author but, more often than not, it's a punt without a large advance because smaller boutique publishers are run by mad aficionados of literature who live on baked beans and dreams and expect their writers to do likewise.

At the same time, a sea change has come over the newspaper business. Some of the best and best-known newspapers, at home and abroad, have stopped making money. Some of them have gone further and are making hellish losses. In the medium term this holds a dread likelihood of consolidation. That's the word for several newspapers getting jammed together with immediate redundancies inside the business and reduced choice for readers. In the short term, it means that newspapers are cutting staff, reducing the numbers of freelances they use and gently suggesting to even their famous columnists that taking a reduced fee would be a graceful gesture towards the survival of this ship and all who sail in her. So the chances of a features' editor looking at a couple of draft columns submitted by you, smacking a hand to their forehead and announcing that you are the next big thing are small.

High hopes are wonderful for motivating a writer, but unreal expectations lead to constant knocks and diminished happiness. Get yourself established as a name in the business. Get yourself established, with editors and producers, as an obliging non-diva who solves, rather than creates problems and, with luck, your ship will come in, you'll get a column and a big advance. Or at least one of the two.

You Have a Day Job and Wouldn't Have the Time

Yes, you would, if you really wanted to. Most people watch television for between three and four hours a night, convincing themselves that: a) they are watching only for two hours at most; b) they have to stay up to date with news, economics and current affairs; and c) they are too tired to do anything else. Giving up television, all on its own, could give you enough time to write a novel inside a year. (It might also lose you weight, since TV-watching is closely related to being fat.)

If you can't bear the thought of missing your favourite soap, then, at the other end of the day, you can get up earlier and write. This is how Anthony Trollope produced countless novels. This is how Bruce Arnold, while delivering on his day job with Independent Newspapers, produced a trilogy of beautiful novels, together with books on art, on political figures and – last year – a book about his own father.

The notion that you will magically become a writer when you cast the permanent and pensionable job from you has nothing to do with reality. You would be out of your tree, in the current climate, to abandon any permanent post in order to become a writer. Put in your eight hours a day. That's forty a week. You know how many you have left? Me neither. But it's a goodly chunk of time. Use it to explore your chances of becoming a full-time writer by doing it as a sideline before you commit yourself to it full-time.

You Would Be Mortified to See Your Name in Print

Why? What are you likely to write that will upset the Gardaí, the Revenue Commissioners or your mother? You can, of course, write under a pseudonym. (Make sure you are upfront with the Revenue Commissioners about it or they, and the Gardaí, will become seriously upset with you and when they put your name in the paper, your mother will be morto.) I've written under at least a dozen names. It must be admitted that it is getting more difficult to write under an alias as branding affects sales of newspapers and books – as you'll find later in this book. But why, anyway, would you start by hiding your light under an alias?

Remember that if the piece you submit covers anything controversial, your editor, whether in a newspaper or a publishing house, will get a severe case of worry rash if you want to use a name that isn't your own. The other complication is that if your feature attracts attention, some radio programme researcher will get on to your editor wanting you on their programme, and no editor, these days, is happy to confess that you're not really the person the paper claimed you were and that you may even be of another gender.

You Don't Know Anybody in the World of Journalism or Publishing and It's Who You Know that Matters

No, it isn't. What matters is who you get to know and how well you meet their professional needs. If a worthwhile feature arrives on the desk of the editor, she's unlikely to go around her office asking if anybody there is the writer's Uncle Bill. She doesn't care whether you're connected. Your being a nobody can be an advantage to the editor, publisher or agent who discovers and promotes you.

You've Never Had Anything Published Before
So what are you waiting for? An invitation?

2

Creating a Writer's Environment

It is a delicious thing to write, to be no longer yourself but to move in an entire universe of your own creating. Today, for instance, as man and woman, both lover and mistress, I rode in a forest on an autumn afternoon under the yellow leaves, and I was also the horses, the leaves, the wind, the words my people uttered, even the red sun that made them almost close their love-drowned eyes. When I brood over these marvellous pleasures I have enjoyed, I would be tempted to offer God a word of thanks if I knew he could hear me. Praised may he be for not creating me a cotton merchant, a vaudevillian, or a wit.

Gustave Flaubert

Being a writer is like being a constantly spinning coin. Heads and tails follow each other endlessly. Heads, you get published. Tails, you get bad reviews. Heads, you get famous. Tails, you lose your privacy. Heads, your book is made into a movie. Tails, they turn your softly nuanced work of art into something so cheaply nasty you would like them to take your name off the credits.

Until you become a writer, the prospect looks like being assumed into heaven: a steady state of bliss. If this were so, writers would be a happy bunch and, although some of them manage to behave as if they are (think Maeve Binchy), most of the hundreds of writers I've interviewed are memorable, as interviewees, for their fury at some aspect of the writer's life that has failed to deliver. Many of them grow to hate the publisher who gave them their first outing with a bitter and twisted passion. Some grow to hate all publishers. Some hate readers for buying in them in paperback rather than in hardback. (Hammond Innes wouldn't autograph anything but hardbacks.) Some hate them for caring about characters the writer created. (Richard Llewellyn, the author of *How Green Was My Valley*, developed into a right-winger in old age, with little sympathy for coalminers losing their jobs.) Some hate the ignoramuses in the media to whom they have to submit themselves in the effort to publicise their latest offering. Most writers cordially loathe the media tour inflicted on them with each emerging title.

All writers dread the critics, because, even if the first book meets with critical acclaim and becomes a big seller, the second book may bomb and when it does, the critics shrug off the reverence with which they greeted the first offering and move directly to a merciless state of mind, fuelled by the inchoate belief that maybe they got sold a pup, first time around.

Most writers do not think through the possible reaction of their friends and family. Some of them – even if the book in question is fiction – will see themselves reflected in the work and they won't like the reflection. Of course, if it's autobiography, not only will it be given for review to someone who hates the writer, but relatives will not hold back their fury at what they see as the author's self-serving insults to the living or the dead. If you choose to publish your memories, you won't have to accuse a relative of unspeakable acts in order to bring down on yourself the wrath of your parents or siblings. Sometimes just being in the book at all makes them feel exposed, exploited and put-upon. Of course, being left out of the book is twice as insulting for some of them.

Anyone planning to make their living as a writer needs to be realistic, not just about the reaction of relatives, critics and readers but about their own potential earnings. Only a handful of writers in this country ever manage to sustain themselves on writing novels or non-fiction books alone. Until relatively recently, the newspapers loved stories of new writers getting 'a £1.5 million advance'. They never went back to find out whether any of the advance was clawed back by the publisher if the second and third books did not justify the expenditure. They never wondered aloud why writers who theoretically were rolling in money would nevertheless find the time to do regular newspaper or radio columns.

The fact is that many non-fiction writers are academics whose day job involves teaching and research and many fiction writers are teachers, nurses, journalists and businesspeople who turn out their short stories or novels in whatever time they have, outside that absorbed by the day job.

The good news is that at different levels of fiction, Irish writers have done remarkably well, in terms of critical response, awards won and copies sold, in recent years. Sebastian Barry, Joseph O'Connor, John Banville, Colm Tóibín and Colum McCann have created international reputations for themselves. So, too, in different genres, have

Marian Keyes, Cathy Kelly, Deirdre Purcell, Patricia Scanlan and Cecelia Ahern. Seamus Heaney is just one of the (living) Irish poets whose works can be found on the shelves of large overseas bookshops. In non-fiction, David McWilliams's very popular works proved he had the zeitgeist by the short and curlies and they are used as source-books about Ireland.

The further good news is that, at least up to the present, the exemption from tax for works of artistic merit, introduced to Ireland by the late Charles J. Haughey, still stands and still makes a hell of a difference to writers whose annual or semi-annual royalty cheques are even more welcome because 40 per cent of them do not have to be forwarded to the Revenue Commissioners the way a goodly percentage of all other earnings has to be.

But – here's the oddity – most writers don't think of themselves as working in a business. Or for money. Many of them would happily have their work published and get no financial return at all. At least in the beginning. In my experience, the wide-eyed enthusiast who refuses to pay any attention to the first contract from a publisher, on the basis that it's a bit beneath them even to consider what percentage of sales will come their way, morphs remarkably quickly into the embittered, put-upon, exploited writer who, a couple of years after they find their way into print, believe they have been hard-done by and complain that Nobody Ever Warned Them.

Whether you write journalism or poetry, fiction or non-fiction, for paper publications or online offerings like the *Huffington Post*, *Slate Magazine* or *Politics.ie*, you are either in it for business reasons or you are in it for vanity. You either want to entertain, move and influence readers professionally or you just like to see your own name in the paper or at the end of your blog. If you're in it for vanity, you have the wonderful freedom of knowing you can write anywhere without looking for money. A blog will do. (See Chapter 15) Or, if you are not computer-literate, a wall. Or the letters pages of the newspaper. Or your FaceBook page. Or Twitter, if you can haiku your life into tweets of no more than a hundred-and-forty characters.

If, on the other hand, you hope either to make a living from your writing or supplement the day job with the odd royalty cheque, let's get you started on becoming a professional writer.

The gadgets you will need to buy we'll get to in a minute, but you already have the most important equipment you need. You may not use your ears properly, yet, but how well or badly you listen will be one of the defining factors that mark you out as a great or good writer or an also-ran.

Successful writers tend to be good listeners. Long before Maeve Binchy published her slew of bestselling novels, she kept newspaper readers entertained with columns based on conversations she overheard. When Maeve listens, she doesn't just listen for content or subject matter. She listens for the rhythms of speech, the phrases that distinguish one person from another, the idea that gets launched and lost.

The more you listen, the more you become aware that attracting and holding anybody's attention is not easy. You can buy guide books to help you find your way through the rules of grammar or help you avoid lurking clichés (have a look at the Bibliography at the end of this book) but if you cannot say what you mean in a way someone else finds interesting, you cannot be a writer. Good writing is not a solo performance. It is a partnership with the reader. Good writing is not a monologue. It is a dialogue with a hidden auditor. Good writing is not a fountain of undirected ideas. It is a way to put insights into other heads and new behavioural possibilities along with them.

Writers who are self-directed nevertheless suffer a rising of the hackles when their work is not fallen upon by the masses. A writer may create sustained monologues which are infinitely satisfying to the writer, but are of no interest to an editor, publisher or reader. Theoretically, the writer should be dead happy that they have reached their main audience but this is rarely the case. Having written for their own delight, writers become irrationally resentful when their writing does not provide the same delight for others as it does for themselves.

The problem is that if you do not observe and listen to others, you cannot know what makes them tick, so you can't talk vividly to them, through your writing. Many of the best writers are intensely shy people who simply want to sit in a corner and hoover up what's useful from around them. Most great writers are also great listeners, no matter whether they are novelists, non-fiction writers, journalists – or, in the case of Abraham Lincoln – a political leader who was also a great writer.

Doris Kearns Goodwin, whose *Team of Rivals* tells the story of Abraham Lincoln's extraordinary people-management, traces his genius for storytelling back to the stories the adult friends of his parents told at night around the fireplace in the log cabin in which he was reared:

> Where Lincoln lived from the age of two until seven stood along the old Cumberland Trail that stretched from Louisville to Nashville. Caravans of

> pioneers passed by each day heading toward the
> Northwest – farmers, peddlers, preachers, each
> with a tale to tell. Night after night, Thomas Lincoln
> would swap tales with visitors and neighbors while
> his young son sat transfixed in the corner.

It was a tutorial in vivid language, much of it profane (the grown-up Lincoln used to tell jokes crude enough to make Tommy Tiernan blush), some of it poetic (he wrote poetry all his life) and some of it rooted in the language of rural America, awash in Biblical references.

It's difficult to be a good writer if you are not a good listener, just as it's difficult to write well if you do not read and have not had reading as a constant habit from childhood. You don't have to have read the contemporaneously approved literature. As long as you read anything, even Enid Blyton or J.K. Rowling, you have a grounding. Cathy Kelly, one of Ireland's most reliable producers of international bestsellers and herself a constant and wide-ranging reader, is always taken aback when she is asked for help by would-be writers who never read. 'I always tell them, if you want to write professionally, you need to read almost professionally,' she says.

Paradoxically, if you have been a hungry reader from your childhood, that very habit can cause you problems when it comes to writing, because beside your bed is a book that really, really must be finished before you get started on the short story for which you have an idea. Or you have purchased a series of non-fiction volumes, the reading of which constitutes necessary research for what you are going to write yourself. Becoming a writer means allocating time to writing. No, I don't mean heading off to a writers' refuge, although you can get information on them from the Arts Council, and some writers swear by them. I mean setting aside time, every day, for writing. The simplest allocation is of the hours before eight in the morning, because it's the one time of the day when nobody outside your family wants anything from you.

If you obey your alarm clock, you can put in two hours of writing before you do your day job. Or one hour, if you want to start small. If you decide to do this, do not kid yourself that getting out of bed at the specified time fulfils your deal with yourself. You have to actually write. Obvious? Yes, to anyone who is not a writer. But writers are born with a gene that at any given time, proposes a range of activities which are more worthy and urgent than writing. Included may be making a cup of coffee, replying to emails, reading newspapers on the web, washing clothes, sorting drawers or just thinking. An hour devoted to writing should be precisely that. It doesn't include coffee-making time.

If you don't have a day job, writing should come before anything else, including cleaning the house. Truman Capote wrote from ten in the morning until noon, believing that those two hours gave him enough time for concentrated work. If a deadline loomed, he would do his morning stint, do something quite different in the afternoon, then return to the desk for a couple of extra hours in the evening.

Lawrence Block, a prolific and stylish thriller writer who has also produced a textbook for fiction writers, warns against the easy option of rising from in front of the computer when the Muse fails to turn up. He maintains that when the Muse doesn't arrive after a long, long time, the amateur writer leaves the writing area, whereas the professional hangs in there.

Nor does your writing time include editing, proofing or rewriting a sentence twenty times to get it perfect. All these are avoidance behaviours. Old newspaper people used to give newcomers a great piece of advice. 'Don't get it right,' they would say. 'Get it written.'

In other words, it's about production before it's about perfection. The desire to achieve perfection may feel virtuous, but it is in fact one of the most self-serving avoidance behaviours used by people who claim they want to be writers. It's a subtle one that kicks in after the would-be hack/novelist/biographer has done all the obvious things that prevent them finding themselves guilty of simple laziness. They get up early, ignore the basket of dirty washing, fight off the temptation to check their inbox, seat themselves at the computer and produce nothing. Their subconscious knows it would be evil to avoid writing by using trivial excuses, but to be overwhelmed by the desire for perfection is OK, you see. Well, you know something? It isn't. Writers write. And then they rewrite. And cut. And submit. That's all there is to it. Perfection doesn't arrive fully grown. It is achieved through constant reworking. Constant reworking can't happen unless you get words down. Sitting there looking at a blank screen won't do it.

Nor does taking a humongous length of time over a piece of writing necessarily improve the quality of the end result. Many of the most productive writers in history wrote against a deadline, with little time to refine what they produced.

According to Tom Raabe, a freelance editor and writer in Denver, Colorado, who wrote a book called *Biblioholism*, the 18th-century writer and lexicographer Dr Johnson was:

...fast and efficient under deadline pressure. He wrote forty-eight printed pages in one sitting once, although it took him all night. He composed seventy lines of poetry in one day and did not write a single line down on paper until he had finished it in his head. His essays for *The Idler* or *The Rambler* were written just prior to press time – he sent the first part in and wrote the remainder while the first part was printing.

More recently, Christopher Buckley, the conservative American writer and editor, maintained that not only is there no correlation between profundity of thought and length of time spent thinking but there is no correlation between excellence of writing and the length of time taken by the writer. Buckley wrote in 2004:

> Every few years, I bring out a collection of previously published work. This of course requires me to reread everything I have done in order to make that season's selections. It transpires that it is impossible to distinguish a column written very quickly from a column written very slowly.

Nor does this apply to journalism alone. Some of the great novelists of history produced millions of words against impossible deadlines, because their survival depended on it. Dr Johnson wrote *Rasselas* in nine days. Balzac, fuelled by coffee, produced sixty books over his lifetime. (Tom Wolfe ironically suggested this might have been because he had no labour-saving devices to 'help' him.)

Of course some writers take forever. Nabokov wrote a hundred and eighty words each day and took between four and five hours to do it. Graham Greene's labours brought forth five hundred words a day.

One school of literary thought holds that the great writer should never touch a keyboard or share a room with a computer, because lashing words into such a receptacle happens too quickly, whereas writing with a fountain pen on hand-hewn Italian paper allows the writer to consider and to develop an almost musical orchestration of thought and hand, productive of shimmering prose. I doubt that Sebastian Barry uses a quill and an ink bottle. I know that Joseph O'Connor doesn't. It's a delightful conceit, but until you have published several novels and perhaps won the Booker Prize, you'd be better advised to slum it by using a computer and setting yourself a more ambitious word count than a hundred and eighty words per day.

Having a word-count goal per day is useful, because it prevents postponement and stops you fooling yourself that because you happen to be physically located in front of a computer and have your fingers on the keys, you are necessarily productive. Writing, like going on a diet, is infinitely postponable. You can put it off until next Monday. Or next January. Or avoid it until you leave your present job. Or do it while seated in front of your PC, repeatedly deleting what you have just written in the belief that it does not add up to the luminous paragraphs which will issue from you as long as you prevent yourself emitting dross. Ever.

Postpone writing and you become a postponer, not a writer. Concentrate on dross-prevention and you may prevent yourself producing anything. Real writers write now.

Newcomers to the trade also need to avoid frighteners. One of the worst frighteners is the description of a writer on the cover of a book. Other writers always seem more interesting, experienced and better qualified to write than you are. Younger, too, and, if you are a woman, other female writers are always prettier and thinner than you are. Be your own man or woman and get on with it.

Give yourself physical and calendar space and insist that they be regarded as sacrosanct by those around you. Set yourself targets. Adopt a 'no excuse' approach to meeting those targets: do not allow yourself to rise from the chair until your word count for the day is complete. Never carry an element of your word count into the next day.

Doing it now guarantees some advantages. Firstly, it means that, after a few weeks, you have something to reject, submit or refine. Secondly, the sense of gratified relief when you meet the day's target is enormous. It's private – nobody else cares that you hit six thousand words. But it is deeply satisfying and gives a splendid sense of entitlement. The rest of the day is yours to do with as you will. Best of all, it's cumulative. If you produce six thousand words a day and work only five days a week, then, at the end of a fortnight, you have the makings of a slenderish paperback.

It helps if you have an environment conducive to writing. Precisely what that environment looks like, sounds like, smells like and feels like depends on the individual writer. Ava McCarthy, whose first thriller, *The Insider,* was published in May 2009 by Harper Collins, did some of her writing sitting in the driver's seat of her thirteen-year-old Mazda as she waited outside her children's school to pick them up. She confided, in an essay published in the *Daily Mail:*

I snatch my mobile writing time whenever I can. In the morning, I park outside the office two hours early and sit there with the laptop on my knees. If I'm lucky, I get a couple of pages written. At lunchtime, I park by the school gates and grab another twenty minutes while I wait for my children. At weekends, I nip out early again and park a hundred yards down the road. Snug in my cocoon, the only noise is the whirring of my laptop and the grinding of my own thoughts. Another chapter done. There are no distractions in a car, no opportunities to procrastinate. No housework, no email, no internet surfing. You can't wander into the kitchen to make a cup of tea or stare into an empty fridge. You're wedged into that bucket seat until either you or the battery gives out.

Ava found that, when she took time out from the day job to write her second book and could afford to set up a home office, it didn't really suit her. The distractions of her home slowed down her progress, and she found herself drawn back to the cramped privacy of her car.

Newsroom journalists learn to filter out the noise of other people's phone calls and shouted conversations in order to concentrate on turning out their story quickly. Similarly, researchers on daily radio programmes working – as most of them do – in cacophonous open-plan offices, develop situational deafness and tunnel vision.

Time spent on seeking to create the perfect writer's environment is usually time wasted. Amazing feats of mental agility, creativity and practicality have occurred under the most adverse circumstances. Perhaps the classic example is the case of a man named David Marshall Williams, who, more than a century ago, was in the US Armed Forces in America's deep south. Williams was not your average malleable character. He lacked the subservience that makes lower ranks popular with officers. More pointedly, he tended to back-answer with profane clarity. By way of punishment, he was sentenced to a form of incarceration consisting of being locked inside a box made of corrugated iron. This did not allow the prisoner to lie down, sit down comfortably, or stand up and ensured that, given the tropical heat, it was a matter of just a few hours before he was in agony.

The general pattern was for soldiers subjected to this kind of punishment to beg for release at the end of the first day, promising good behaviour in future. Truly obdurate prisoners lasted as long as thirty-six hours before caving in.

At the end of the first day's torture, Williams's hot box was opened to allow food and water to be handed to him. Asked if he wanted to apologise for whatever crime had landed him there, he fixed the questioner with a look of silent contempt and was duly sealed up again. The following day, he sweated in the harsh darkness but again, at nightfall, refused to speak. Days moved into weeks, and eventually, when it became obvious to the army authorities that he would die rather than give in, he was released. It took him some considerable time to learn to walk again. His fellow soldiers were curious to find out how he had survived what he had been through and what he felt about the darkness, the heat and the rigidly defined space.

He shrugged. He had, he told them, been far too busy to notice much of the misery. Too busy? Yes, he told them.

He had been too busy planning the innards of a gun he had wanted to build for some time and doing the mathematics of scale and placement. That work was now complete, thanks to the uninterrupted stay in the tiny prison, and he could have the gun manufactured as soon as he got out of the military. He was right. In due course, the gun – the carbine rifle – became one of the biggest sellers in the arms trade and its inventor was nicknamed Carbine Williams.

None of us would want to create anything, whether it be a gun or a novel, under such circumstances, but more than guns have been designed in the heads of prisoners. Several works of literature have been produced in brutal surroundings. Alexander Solzhenitsyn 'wrote' poetry and prose in the Gulag without always having paper on which to write down his drafts. He would think out several lines and commit them to memory. The next day, he would tag further lines on to the base, learning the aggregate poem by rote. It was endlessly tedious and highly effective. Once released, he was able to transcribe from memory a considerable volume of material.

In the concentration camps of the Holocaust, the same thing happened. Prisoners painted, carved and wrote. Tzvetan Todorov, Director of Research at the Centre National de Recherches in Paris, has found countless examples of this urge to create, even in the most inhuman conditions, and credits it to the sense, among the prisoners, that 'no life is lived in vain if it leaves behind some trace of itself, some story that, when added to the countless other stories by which we know who we are, contributes even if in the smallest way, to making the world a more harmonious and more perfect place.'

The urge to create accompanied Oscar Wilde when he walked into prison in Reading in 1895 following his disastrous libel action against Lord Queensberry. His embellished life as a society favourite was over. He was frequently sick. He was forced to do hard labour. He suffered a dearth of reading materials so dire that he later told a friend he had developed a sad skill in reading other people's newspapers upside down, in order to gain illicit access to what was in the prison officers' papers. Writing materials were similarly restricted. Issued with a single numbered page, he could fill it with prose or poetry but was then forced to relinquish it at the end of the day. There was no possibility of holding ten pages of, say, a poem. Despite all this – or perhaps because of it – Wilde wrote the anguished and untypically simple *The Ballad of Reading Gaol* during the period.

The brutal truth is that if you want to call yourself a writer, you have to write even when the wind is in the wrong direction, the miseries are on you, the bailiffs are at the door and the bruises are turning from purple to dirty yellow.

You cannot publish excuses and you cannot hope that a stroke of good fortune will get you to the point where, beside 'Occupation' on your passport, you put 'Writer.'

It's a bit like the comment made by the world-famous Irish amateur golfer, Joe Carr, when someone congratulated him on his luck in winning a tournament. 'I am lucky, all right,' Carr said. 'And you know what? The more I practise, the luckier I get.'

The same applies to writing. The more regularly you force yourself to write, the easier writing will become. You do not have to have a book-lined study, a super-fast PC, access to LexisNexis or a beaker of great coffee.

Whenever you have money, invest in the best technology around. Not necessarily the newest technology. It's safer to wait until something becomes the norm before you buy it, especially if it's expensive. Sometimes, technology is invented slightly before its time. Fifteen years ago, e-books were available for download on to a hand-held device. I bought one. It was a waste of money. Not until the Kindle and the Sony e-book reader did the technology match the times. Up to that point, it was clunky.

The most essential technology for any writer is the simplest and cheapest. It is the flash-drive, which allows you to save everything that matters on your computer each week to a tiny device you can store in another place, so that if your computer gets stolen, burned or broken, you do not find yourself mourning 100,000 words, ready for sub-division into the chapters of a novel.

Buy a good chair, a comfortable desk, a good computer and a flash drive, if you can afford them. Buy a computer and a flash drive even if you can't afford them. If you live beside a house where the teenager is learning the drums and you find you can't filter out the noise by sheer force of will, buy ear plugs. No – not those Bose earphones that electronically even out all noise and feed you either an artificial silence or soft music. Just mushy malleable foam or wax bundles, obtainable in your local pharmacy, which you shove in your ears to exclude sound. They will do the job, albeit less glamorously.

Tell the adults who share your home that during particular hours, unless Barack Obama arrives at the front door or flames start licking at the kitchen ceiling, you are not to be disturbed. (And even then, they need to find out what Obama wants and try to quench the flames before invading your office.) Working at home is, for most of a writer's non-writer friends, a contradiction in terms. They figure you will be bored and need cheering up. That they have something they really, really shouldn't have bought and want your opinion on it. That they're thinking of hypnosis for the weight they keep piling on and want you to do it with them. Never mind the reason, they arrive at your door.

'I know you're supposed to be working,' they say, laughing lightly at the very possibility that what you do could be considered to be real work. Meanwhile, your inner voice says 'Whattya mean, *supposed* to be working? I *was* working.'

'But I knew you wouldn't mind if I popped in,' they go on, stepping past you into your home. Your inner voice minds terribly. It begins to use four-letter words. But you still find yourself retreating down the hall and working out whether you'll make real coffee or instant.

'I won't stay a minute,' they conclude, planting themselves in your most comfortable chair so determinedly, you know you'll be lucky if you get them out before lunchtime.

Every visitor to a writer who works at home makes of themselves an exception. They have enough empathy to figure that anyone arriving on your doorstep is not a good thing, from your point of view, and they join you happily in despising those time-wasters. They themselves, however, are uniquely different and they expect you to welcome them in that light. You have to learn to stand at the door and refuse to let them in.

'You know I'd love to have a cup of coffee with you,' you should say, 'but I'm at such a crucial place in my writing, if I even interrupt it for two minutes, it'll be lost. I will text you later. I know you will understand.'

In a weird coincidence, just after I had written that last piece of advice, I heard a knocking on the kitchen window and found a man standing in the field at the back, leaning over the fence. I opened the window and he told me he was my second cousin who had spent the last forty years in Africa. Despite the fact that I had never met him before the forty-year absence, I would normally have invited him in, but, my resolve stiffened by having had to address the issue, I told him I hoped he would have a great time while he was home and he would forgive me, but I was in the throes of writing a book. He was very pleasant about it, which made it worse. But I'm still writing, aren't I?

You contribute to your ruthless devotion to the writer's craft if you fix your mobile phone so it goes directly to messages and arrange a landline emergency code with your nearest and dearest, so they can ring, say, once, cut themselves off and then ring directly thereafter. But make sure your nearest and dearest understands what constitutes an emergency. SuperValu not having any cooked chicken, which they agreed to pick up, is not an emergency. They're grown up. They need to learn to improvise.

Blackmail works well with children: 'You know I promised to take you to the ice-skating rink? Well, if I don't get this feature off to the newspaper today, I won't have enough money to do it and you'll have to stay at home.'

You have a choice. You can be popular with friends, colleagues and family. You can be the person who can always be relied on to dig everybody else out, the person who is always good for a laugh, one of the gang. Or you can be a writer. Your choice.

Make up your mind, work out your methods, and stick with it. And don't waste any time trying to create the perfect ambience, where the walls are lined with morocco-bound books, soft music filters through an iPod station and the view out the window is of pastoral peace. As long as you're not freezing or being constantly talked at, anywhere is a good environment for a writer.

3

COURSES AND GROUPS AND HOW-TO BOOKS

Credentialism – tying good jobs to diplomas –
made a university degree into a meal ticket.
Charles Derber, William A. Schwartz and Yale Magrass,
Power in the Highest Degree

The majority of the published writers in the nineteenth century and the first half of the twentieth century did not have degrees in English, Media, Film, Communications or Creative Writing. Many of the published writers in the latter half of the twentieth century and the first decade of the twenty first don't have those credentials, either.

A primary degree is now the same as the Leaving Certificate used to be: a basic qualification for any kind of employment. So persuaded is society of the pivotal importance of higher education that, as the first recession of the twenty-first century deepened, the Irish government provided funds for unemployed individuals to go to university to get such degrees. Many unemployed graduates went back to college to do PhDs or Masters, or, in some cases, second Masters. This might make sense if they want to be a world-class physicist or electronics engineer. If, on the other hand, they want to be a writer, it makes no sense at all. Universities tend to teach students in these disciplines how to analyse and deconstruct material rather than how to create it.

Long before the recession, however, major growth in creative writing courses at third level had been evident globally. In 1975, for example, fifty-two degree programmes in creative writing were offered by American universities. By 2005, that number had grown to 300. Charles McGrath, a former editor of *The New York Times Book Review*, wrote in that paper on 14 April 2009 that, as a result, it is arguable that a majority of American writers now make most of their living by teaching others how to write, rather than by writing themselves:

> In the 1940s and 50s Americans who wanted to become writers went to Paris. Now they go to Palo Alto or Iowa City. And except for being more expensive than Paris, writing school doesn't seem to have harmed these generations of writers, despite the naysayers who complain that the programs turn out competent but unoriginal practitioners of whatever style happens to be in vogue. To judge from various memoirs and testimonials, most writing school alumni would probably say their time in the classroom helped.

Whether it is possible to teach a student to become a writer has always been a topic for debate. 'Are writers born or made?' is one of those pointless discussions like the cats versus dogs argument, which allows the fearless repetition of unevidenced prejudices going back hundreds of years. Since my company, the Communications Clinic, offers a range of writing programmes, most of them directed to business but some related to creative writing, I should come down firmly on the 'writers can be made' side of the debate, but I cannot do so.

It is certainly possible, through a training course, to get someone out of their own way by kicking the worst of their bad habits out of them. The first time I provided this service was on a Basics of Journalism course more than thirty years ago, run by Fr. Brian D'Arcy for mostly religious students in the old Catholic Communications Centre in Booterstown Avenue in Dublin.

Perhaps twenty-five men and women took part in the course, which lasted three weeks. It was intensely practical. Each of them had to write reports, features, profiles, radio scripts and press releases. They learned to work quickly and accurately. Some of them were enormously talented. All of them enjoyed the experience so much that, at the end, we had difficulty persuading them to go home. They knew how much more skilful they were and promised the tutors that they would forward clippings of their published material. When – finally – we were on our own, tidying up the training rooms, Brian and I speculated as to how many clippings we'd get. None, was the answer. That is not to say that none of the trainees managed to get anything published. Years later, I picked up a book written by one of them. Even though they showed boundless talent and had learned saleable skills, the majority never put them to the test.

People go on courses for all sorts of reasons. Some participants on a training course will be chronic course-goers, just as some students are chronic students. It doesn't matter how many degrees they have or how old they are, they prefer the student life to anything else. Some participants want to prove something to themselves and surviving the course provides that proof. Some genuinely believe that they will concentrate on writing after the course but what actually happens is that the cares and riches and pleasures of daily life get in their way.

Occasionally, someone goes on a writing course and ends up demotivated and humiliated, either because they realise that they simply cannot produce work to order, because the course tutor is not helpful to their particular talent, or because they could not withstand the humiliation of having their work shared and commented upon by others. It was ever thus. More than seventy years ago, Dorothea Brande, herself a teacher of creative writing, penned a warning for teachers on this issue (in *Becoming a Writer*, which was first published in 1934):

> I think that holding up the work of each pupil in class for the criticism of the others is a thoroughly pernicious practice, and it does not become harmless simply by allowing the manuscript to be read without assigning its authorship publicly. The ordeal is too trying to be taken with equanimity, and a sensitive writer can be thrown out of his stride deplorably by it, whether or not the criticism is favorable. It is seldom that the criticism is favorable, when a beginner is judged by the jury of his peers. They seem to need to demonstrate that, although they are not yet writing quite perfectly themselves, they are able to see all the flaws in a story which

is read to them, and they fall upon it tooth and fang. Until self-confidence arises naturally, and the pupil asks for group criticism, his work should be treated as utterly confidential by the teacher. Each will have his own rate of growth and it can only go on steadily if not endangered by the setbacks that come from embarrassment and self-consciousness.

Just as ill-judged savagery is harmful to a newcomer, so is ill-judged flattery, which can often arise, in group situations, from a self-preservation instinct. It's a bit like my brother-in-law Peter's claim that whenever he goes to have his teeth looked at, his first move is to catch the dentist by his private parts and say, 'We're not going to hurt each other, are we?' In much the same way, course participants send an unspoken message to each other: 'If I don't say anything horrible about you, you won't say anything horrible about me, sure you won't?' In consequence, each participant's self-esteem is pointlessly boosted by praise motivated by self-preservation on the part of the person delivering the plaudits.

Now and again, particularly with overseas holiday courses, participants admire one another's tiny written offerings, discover depths within them that are not actually present, and concentrate on having sun-sand-and-sex relationships they convince themselves are on a higher intellectual level than would have happened if they had just gone to a resort of beer-drinking twenty-somethings in Lanzarote. A minority on every course come out of it with what they warmly confirm are more acute insights into the business/art/craft of writing and are content that, at some stage in the future, these insights will come into play.

If you go on a writing course, be the exception. Be the one who hoovers up everything useful and is a constant annoyance because you ask the extra question and do not waste time on the social life attached to the programme. (Let's face it. It's tough enough to live with one would-be writer – you. Why would you want to complicate your life by adding another? You may quote me Jonathan and Faye Kellerman. I'll raise you Hemingway and his wife, war correspondent Martha Gelhorn, plus Scott Fitzgerald and Zelda.)

Of course, before you get down to being the exception, you have to pick your course carefully. Any good writing-skills programme, whether devoted to business writing or the basics of journalism or creative writing, should be 80 per cent practical. You should have to produce the goods, against a deadline, every day. Too many programmes are provided by writers or journalists who have run out of writing steam, and who are into their anecdotage. They may be highly entertaining with their stories of what happened to them when they used to work for Vinnie Doyle, or fascinating with their accounts of what it was like to be edited by Douglas Gageby, but entertainment is not skills-building, and the bigger the personality of the writer (or former writer) the less likely they are to concentrate on each student enough to draw from them all they can deliver.

That said, the course should definitely be led by someone who has been published. Ideally within the recent past. Former broadcaster Liam Nolan, for example, ran a writer's course in Loughrea which was much praised by several of those who graduated from it into being published. It was undoubtedly informed by the fact that he had published ten books, but also, and arguably more importantly, by his continuing to write.

Nolan published his eleventh book when he was seventy-seven. Good reports also emanate from NUIG's creative writing programmes presented by the considerably younger Fred Johnston, also a published novelist and poet.

The market for the written word changes radically roughly every seven years, so you need a tutor who is up to speed with the mechanics that currently apply. Good writing-skills courses should have more than one tutor, for several reasons, not least of which is the incapacity of any one tutor to 'click' with each of the participants. Cream rises to the top very quickly on a writing course, and the temptation, for any tutor, is to concentrate on the people who are producing it. But a range of trainers will ensure that the slow learners come through, too, and that it's not only the easy, obvious talents who shine.

Be clear, when you go on a training course, that if it's any good, you will develop an intense relationship with at least one of the tutors. Remember, you are going to be under pressure, you are going to be trying to explore your own soul or get to the essence of, say, someone you have been told to interview.

This makes you vulnerable, not just to criticism but, much more importantly, to praise. Your trainers have to be committed to identifying what you are good at while challenging any aspect of your writing which is mediocre. The end result, on any good training course, is that you half-fall in love with the situation and at least one of the trainers.

In this context, it is difficult to understand that although a professional trainer may spot a gem in something you write which makes you feel that only you and the trainer, out of the entire world, are on the same wavelength, that's the trainer's job, and three weeks later, when you meet them, they may have a) difficulty getting your name right, because they meet so many students in any one month, and b) no recollection of the discovery which – to you – was and is so crucially important. The fact that they have forgotten you does not falsify what they said about your work; it just means they have other things and people on their mind, as do you.

It is important also to understand that no matter what claims are made by the course-providers, the key to your success, post-course, is you. They are not going to act as your agents, although, in the past, some questionable tutors who had been in media or publishing used to pull in favours for each participant, so almost everybody involved had one piece published during or directly after the programme, thereby allowing the course providers to claim that '98 per cent of our students are published within a year of undertaking the programme'.

The cost to you as an individual of a fortnight's Basics of Journalism or Creative Writing Course can vary from €500 to €5000. It can be even more expensive if it is run in a sunshine resort or an overseas university and I know of no infallible way to ensure you are not going to be ripped off. On the other hand, while no single course can guarantee to equip you to be a writer, any half-decent course can provide attention, encouragement and a little professional guidance, and since these three are thin on the ground, it is a win/win for the novice writer.

Readers' and writers' groups are another way of learning about literature and writing. They often represent a cheaper option than a training course. Your local library is a good source of information on these kinds of group.

Readers' groups agree to read a particular book within a set period of time and discuss it. Because of the growing numbers of these groups, internationally, many paperbacks now have interviews with the author at the back, which concentrate on precisely the kinds of issues readers' groups tend to explore. Writers' groups agree to produce and share work, whether on a particular theme or within a specific genre. The idea of a group of would-be writers sitting around and criticising something you wrote may not appeal to you. (It sure as hell wouldn't appeal to me.) But, particularly in America, an increasing number of first novels carry an acknowledgement of the help of members of a reading or writing group, who are credited by the author with encouragement and judicious suggestions. So it's a possibility to be considered at least, as a way of getting someone who is not too close to you to give you an opinion on your output. Although they might want to help, often those close to us cannot stand back and approach our work as dispassionately as they would if it was offered for their perusal by a complete stranger.

Stephen King's approach to getting an external take on your work is worth considering too:

> Show your work to a number of people – ten, let us say. Listen carefully to what they tell you. Smile and nod a lot. Then review what was said very carefully. If your critics are all telling you the same thing, about some facet of your story – a plot twist that doesn't work, a character who rings false, stilted narrative or half a dozen other possibilities – change that facet. It doesn't matter if you really liked that twist or that character; if a lot of people

are telling you something is wrong with your piece, it is. If seven or eight of them are hitting on that same thing, I'd still suggest changing it. But if everyone – or even most everyone – is criticising something different, you can safely disregard what all of them say.

Having a mentor or supportive critic or confidant is a help but no more than that. Don't ever fall into the habit of talking about your work rather than working at it. It doesn't matter that you have had your soul enlarged by editorial discussion. What matters is the quantity and quality of words produced and, in due course, sold.

Ultimately, being a writer is a lonely experience. You are on your own. Even if you're part of a writers' group or attending a course, even if you're surrounded by other writers inputting material into their computers, you are still essentially on your own at the point where you commit your thoughts to a hard disc or paper. This can be a challenge. Too often, writers have helped themselves to meet that challenge with a shot of alcohol. Drugs, alcohol and cigarettes appear to aid creativity in the short term. In the long term, both are the road to no town. In fact, if you plan to make your living from writing, remember that it's a job demanding considerable stamina and make sure you get enough sleep and exercise.

Finally, let's look at books that set out to help you become a writer. When novelist and literary critic Malcolm Bradbury agreed to write an introduction to a reissue of Dorothea Brande's *Becoming a Writer*, he summed up the value of such texts:

Most are full of goodwill and bread-and-butter advice and often have a fair degree of practical use: teaching a would-be author the basic rules of storytelling and genre, exploring the organisational problems and difficulties that arise in the writing of novels, short stories, poems and plays. As you'd guess, the best are usually those written by distinguished writers themselves, the people who have learned the hard way and produced the finest results. But on the whole it's an uninspired genre, and the biggest danger is that it teaches mechanical rules, simple practices, conventional routines – just those rules that are broken by any writer of originality. The essence of serious writing is that it's not a struggle to repeat what others have done, but a struggle not to…

The Bibliography on page 223 includes the book to which Bradbury wrote the introduction, as well as others, by writers as different as John Steinbeck, Stephen King and Rita Mae Browne. Reading what other writers have to say about writing can be fascinating and can relieve the anxiety every writer experiences. No guide to writing can turn you into a writer. But if it arrives at the point where you are already on your way, it may help you to avoid obvious pitfalls.

That is what happened Marian Keyes. Nearly seventeen years ago, her father gave her a Christmas present. It was a copy of an earlier edition of the book you are currently reading. 'Marian, let 1993 be a lovely Christmas and have a story published by 1994. Lots of love and success, Dad,' read the inscription.

Marian was relieved to find, reading a bit through the first chapter, that the book was mostly, as she saw it, commonsense. She remembers:

> There was such a mystique about writing and being published. I didn't have a clue. It was like this locked room you had to have a secret password to get into. Most people think they have to have a family tradition of having been writers; that if your parents haven't been published, you haven't a hope. I suppose these days, with blogging, that gives people more freedom. Nevertheless, it's one thing to blog, but it's another to write and get paid. I really thought it was great to have things demystified. I sent some of my short stories to Kate Cruise O'Brien at Poolbeg and said I had started writing a novel. She told me she liked them, but that sort stories don't sell in book form, especially by an unknown. For me, they were the foothills of novels. So I wrote four chapters of a novel and sent them to her. She loved them. I still have the letter from her. And they became my first novel.

Marian neatly sums up the strengths and weaknesses of how-to-write books. This one won't make you into a writer. Or guarantee publication. But it may demystify the context, so you can get on with the main job of writing, without the excuse of ignorance. It is as simple and terrifying as that.

4

Making a Living

*A living is made by selling something that every-
body needs at least once a year.*
  Yes, Sir.
  *And a million is made by producing something
that everybody needs every day.*
  *You artists produce something that nobody
needs at any time.*

Thornton Wilder

If you want to write for yourself alone and never seek publication, this book must already be irritating you. Because it is
not meant for someone who sees writing only as a means of
private creativity and self-expression. It is meant for someone
who wants to make a living, or part of a living, through the
written word.

A couple of years ago, I sideswiped a politician in the
weekly column I write for the *Irish Examiner*. It wasn't much
of a sideswipe. But it drove the young woman involved right
around the twist. I know this because the day after the column
appeared, her response seethed into my inbox. Screen after
screen of fury erupted when I opened her mail. At the end of

it, I instinctively did a word count. Her reply to my column was double the word count of the opinion piece that had maddened her.

I wrote civilly back to her to offer her some free communications advice:

> Waste not your time, in future, writing to columnists who annoy you. Attack a columnist directly and he or she tends to get shirty and defensive. Columnists, in my experience, rarely come out the following week in sackcloth and ashes, announcing that they were totally arseways the previous week and they have now repented. The thing to do is get good and mad – and get money and profile out of it. Take this email you've sent to me, change it from being a one-to-one complaint into a condemnation of what I wrote, reduce it by half its length and get it to the editor of the *Examiner* in the next two hours with a covering note demanding right of reply to what I wrote.

This utterly floored her. She came back to me, worried that this approach would do me harm. I explained that any editor would prefer to have reaction, negative or positive, than silence in response to a columnist's work. (Editors are less happy when they get solicitors' letters threatening libel action, but any form of reaction short of that, even a savage attack on their own columnists, they experience as a form of reinforcement.) In addition, as far as editors are concerned, controversy is good, so they welcome, in the interests of balance, a response to criticisms of an individual, political party, sectoral group or business. Yet many readers whose sensibilities become inflamed as a result of something they read in a newspaper tend to think first of contacting the writer. The form of contact varies. I got a death threat with a drawing of a tombstone from a well-known criminal as a result of a light-hearted piece I did about him for a newspaper. So far, he has not delivered on the threat but it caused great excitement in the newspaper, where it was opened in error. The features' editor telephoned me to apologise and to explain what kind of letter it was. I laughed and told her I'd haunt her if he did me in, since it was she – not me – who had come up with the idea for the offending feature. Ignoring this, she told me firmly that her newspaper had rules around an issue like this and that she and the editor were on their way to Store Street Garda Station to bring the letter to the attention of the Garda Siochana.

In due course, two detectives visited me in my office to brief me on their investigation and give me good advice on protecting myself. One of them probed for emotional response. How, he wanted to know, did I feel about this? I dithered. It was clear he expected my knickers to be in a twist and for a moment, I considered letting on that they were. But I didn't have the time, because we were in the process of setting up a brand-new business in the teeth of a recession.

'I'm really grateful to the two of you,' I said. 'But I can't devote much time to death threats at the moment. If he really wants to terminate me, I just hope he does it efficiently.'

Death threats are rare, at least in my experience, but most writers of opinion pieces, sooner or later, get what we call the green-ink letter. Nobody knows why these letters tend to be written in bright emerald ink but it's either that or purple.

Handwritten. On ruled paper. With heavy underlining of sections the writer really, really, really wants the recipient to register. Plus several postscripts. And, if the letter-writer is particularly fraught, afterthoughts up the side and across the top.

Green-ink letters usually come from people with strong religious convictions and are provoked by their belief that the writer is a) against the Pope and b) against God. It is a mistake to respond to these letters, because the letter-writer cannot be mollified and will be further provoked by your response, no matter how emollient.

Death threats and green-ink letters apart, most of the correspondence reaching newspaper writers from readers is lucid and authoritative. Sometimes it is so tightly argued that it would make you revise your original mindset on the topic. At *The Sunday Times*, the features' editor or the editor routinely scans letters sent to columnists on the newspaper and contacts some senders to say, in effect, 'Why don't you tinker with this so it's addressed to the editor rather than the columnist, and send it to us for publication, because you are making interesting points and it's a shame to confine them to one person.' Many of the letter-writers immediately agree. Which at least gets their views more widely shared.

However, the person who writes either to a columnist or to the editor of a newspaper for publication is rarely a professional writer. When a professional writer gets riled by something they read, they hit their keyboard immediately, but their stinging rebuttal takes the form of a feature, rather than a letter. A feature has two advantages over a letter. If accepted, it will appear on the general pages of the paper rather than the letters page. The letters page in any newspaper draws its own dedicated readership; and, contrariwise, many newspaper buyers read only the news and features and couldn't be bothered reading the letters page. The second advantage is that you get paid for a feature, whereas you do not get paid for a letter to the editor, generally speaking, although some newspapers and other publications give prizes for the best letter of the week.

When I used to edit women's magazines, I was startled to find that some correspondents would send in as many as six letters at a time, on different topics, all carefully tailored to the evident bias of the publication, in order to win the small cash prizes, which they regularly did. It did not seem to strike them that a bottle of plonk or a tenner was considerably less in value than the cheque which would have issued if they had crafted their thoughts to run on the features' pages.

It's about purpose. If articulating your views on a certain subject is more important to you than making money, then an endless supply of markets opens up to you, starting with the text messages read out on radio programmes. You can Twitter – and join the overwhelming majority of its users, who, according to a study done by Pear Analytics, tweet nothing more than 'pointless babble.' If you want to be taken more seriously and want to input at greater length, then you can move from tweeting to writing a blog (of which more in Chapter 15). Sometimes, people who are very busy with their day job and have no great urge to write for money, use amateur writing as a hobby. I have a friend – a gifted and costly photographer – who gets his kicks by writing pithy two- or three-line letters to *The Irish Times*. He figures on the letters page at least once a month and in some cases his offerings are entertaining, informing, questioning and educative. He is a professional photographer and an amateur writer, who wants to entertain, inform, question or educate.

While the professional writer may have something in common with my amateur friend, the essential difference is that writer's secondary purpose may be to entertain, inform, question or educate, while their primary purpose is to get paid. Getting paid has obvious advantages, like being able to eat, pay the phone bill and buy the school uniforms for the children. For the aspirant writer, it may also have the advantage of allowing them to ditch the day job.

Now, I know this runs counter to the traditional image of writers. Writers are supposed to be above earthly considerations like budgets. They think on higher things so they don't need much money. They live in garrets, don't they? And how much does your average garret cost?

The valorisation of writers by reference to their level of commercial ignorance is history. Writers who do not regard what they're doing as a professional activity worth financial reward end up embittered because they handle money and contracts badly.

In theory, the best way to approach writing as a professional activity is to put a value on your time and work from the outset and stick to it. In practice, particularly during bad economic times, this is not necessarily the best place to start.

Markets are so tight, particularly in freelance journalism, that three objectives may take precedence over the immediate making of dosh:

1. Getting experience
2. Getting visibility
3. Getting credibility

Achieving those three objectives, in a recession, may mean working for free. It may mean bartering your time for some training within an organisation. This gets dressed up in phrases like 'internships' and 'work experience'. It has a lot going for it, as an approach.

Work experience or internship has contracted in one area and expanded in another. It has contracted within newspapers. Some still offer the opportunity for a student or recent graduate to come in for four or six weeks during which they get a real sense of how a modern newspaper is put together. However, in the past, if the intern showed considerable energy and promise, there was a good chance that they might be offered a junior staff position at the end of their free labour. This is no longer the case in almost any newspaper in Ireland. Most of them restructured over the past ten years and several have restructured more than once, offering exit packages to staff in order to reduce their overhead. In this context, an internship offers work experience and nothing more.

The same difficulty about gaining a long-term job out of it applies right across the board, but, since 2007, work experience in the private sector generally has expanded. Many companies, including publishing companies, now offer lengthy internships to graduates. They can learn the ropes, but – in the current economic freeze – their chances of getting staffed at the end of their apprenticeship are slim and their chances of getting paid even slimmer. Some communications consultancies do variations on this theme. If you go for such a long-term internship, get the terms and conditions in writing in advance, so that you are guaranteed at least a variety of work and perhaps some specific training during your time with the company.

Back in the last recession, a third-level student who did a work experience month in my company stayed with us, working his way up through the (admittedly thin) ranks so that he eventually became managing director. A senior consultant in the Public Relations Clinic within our present company started with us in the same way. Making yourself indispensable, as a contributing worker and as a personality, can work even in the most extraordinarily difficult situations.

Even if you do not get taken on to the staff in the PR company or media outlet to which you give your time, *gratis*, you may gain from the weeks or months you spend with it. At the negative end, you may realise that this business is not for you. It may be too stressful, too repetitive or too top-heavy, so that you do not see yourself getting into anything more interesting than floor-sweeping, message-taking and coffee-making before 2020.

More positively, work experience can help you to make the transition from the theory of third level to the practicalities of the workplace. It can teach you how to write quickly under pressure. It can kick-start you into a more active ambition. It's up to you. It's completely up to you. Even if they are busy and preoccupied, the professionals around you will quickly spot whether or not you have potential.

In just one week last year, the Communications Clinic welcomed two people doing work experience. The young man was highly educated, experienced, perfectly dressed, confident and personable. The young woman was a first-year student with no experience who smiled silently and looked like she'd been dressed for a third birthday party.

On the Wednesday of their first week with us, at seven-thirty in the morning, our receptionist took a call and announced, to the five staff members present, that one of the two work experience people had got herself a job and wouldn't be with us any more. A dismayed silence greeted this. Then someone asked which of the two she meant. The male, she responded.

'Thanks be to Jasus,' came the chorused reaction.

Of course we were delighted that he had got a solid job offer and we wished him well. But we wished him well anywhere but around us, because within those first two days he had revealed himself to be a world-class pain in the arse, mainly because he didn't know what he didn't know. He didn't know the difference between the irreverent humour with which we greet our clients and straightforward impertinence. He didn't know that in any open office, it's up to newcomers to create their own invisible cubicles, rather than involve themselves in every conversation-cluster. He didn't know how to spell and didn't think it mattered. He didn't know that it isn't the job of the girls to bring coffee to the rest of us. We hadn't had the time to discuss any of this, but each of us had been doing some private teeth-grinding.

The first-year student, on the other hand, was not just diligent but quietly diligent. She didn't simply do the task set her: she kept her eyes open and silently sorted other obvious tasks. She quickly picked up on our corporate culture (which relies heavily on teasing) and gave as good as she got. At the end of her time with us, we had to force ourselves to be responsible and not try to persuade her to abandon her degree and simply come to work for us. And we missed her and constantly quoted her as a model work-experiencer when she went back to university.

If you decide to do work experience in an organisation

related to writing, while you are still at school or college or after you have been made redundant, bring your energy, discretion and commitment to learn with you, and leave your personal needs at home.

The 'work experiencer' everybody dreads is the one who dutifully goes through the motions for a week and then seeks an appointment with the MD, head of training, features' editor or series producer to ask their guidance about how to become Mary Wilson, Tim Vaughan, Ed Mulhall or Charlie Bird – immediately. This is not the way to the top: it may well be the way to the bottom, as the mid-level people who have been asked to take care of you resent your queue-jumping.

On work experience, you arrive early and leave late. You watch and listen and shut up. You do not talk about what you have witnessed in your local the night before. You turn your mobile phone off except at coffee and lunch breaks. If you have nothing to do, you find something to do.

The man I mentioned earlier, who later became my managing director, found out, during his few weeks of work experience, that the cleaning lady was on holiday. He took over her job, so, barging into the Ladies quite late one evening, I collided with him and a vacuum cleaner. It's amazing, the hidden depths you discover in a lad who can relationship-build with a vacuum cleaner. The fact that he later turned out to write like an angel and to have a genius for relationship-making with clients (he did not, fortunately, confine himself to working the vacuum cleaner) was a bonus.

When you are on work experience, or do a deal with a magazine, newspaper, radio or TV station or communications consultancy, do not annoy the powers that be or your temporary colleagues by canvassing for a job. You are not there to solve your problems. You are there to solve their problems. If you do it well, and if, at the same time, you concentrate on learning everything you can learn, you will come out of it with useful contacts, boosted confidence and a raised skill level. Useful contacts should not be abandoned. As you leave, ask the person who has the best understanding of your capability to give you a reference. Stay in contact with them after you leave, ideally in a way that is useful to them, rather than to you. Draw their attention to an upcoming tender with a company or government department you know something about. Send them a link to a useful feature. Not every day or every week, and make sure the communication reeks of bright buoyancy, even if that's not how you feel.

A month or several months working for nothing or for expenses can give you experience and something on your CV which may be useful, especially if you're starting out fresh from school or college. This time doesn't often give you visibility – in other words, get you known outside the circle of those employing you.

Visibility is a strange thing. You may not get work without it but you might lose work because of too much of it. If a radio producer doesn't know you from a brick in the wall, they may not feel inclined to take a risk on you as a scriptwriter. On the other hand, if you appear everywhere, you can become over-exposed, a condition most readily diagnosed by potential employers who haven't got the money to make it worth your while to sell your services exclusively to them but who still resent the fact that you flog your wares elsewhere.

The visibility you want was summed up by Bunny Carr, my first boss. 'You want to be just well enough known,' Bunny said, 'that when you walk through the open-plan offices in

RTÉ television or radio, someone glances up from their desk and says, 'Hey – the very man!' or, 'The very woman!'"

To make a living from writing in Ireland, this is the level of visibility you need: enough fame for potential publishers of your work to see you as meeting a need they have.

Once your competence is proven by publication, and editors and readers alike begin to recognise your byline, you may want to find out what you should be paid, as opposed to accepting whatever the publication decides you're worth. You should never start with the money you're going to ask for. A happy writing life results from doing what you want to do, first, and getting paid for it into the bargain.

One of the ways to find out the going rate is to seek information from the National Union of Journalists about freelance rates. This will give you some idea of the amount of money newspapers, magazines or radio programmes are prepared to pay for 600, 800 or 1000 words. What the NUJ has managed to negotiate for its freelance members has two caveats attached to it. The first is that the freelance rate laid down by the NUJ is always a minimum. It is the rate below which no union member should work. Consequently, it is on the low side. Secondly, the rate applies to the union's members. If you are not a member of the union, you are on your own, and liable to meet with a derisive laugh if you quote union rates, no matter how modest they are, to an editor who knows you to be a newcomer.

The great difficulty for writers when it comes to deciding what they are worth is that so much of their creative and analytical power goes on other things. When you ask a group of, say, university students going through a journalism or media or PR degree programme what they would like to earn as writers, they get all shifty with embarrassment. That is partly because so many of them, these days, regard writing as the block-laying, boring bit of media professionalism and would much rather present TV fashion programmes than dig up facts and put them in readable order. It's also because so many of them assume they will get a staff job on one of the major newspapers or in RTÉ and be paid a good solid stipend without having to negotiate with anybody for it: you join the mother ship, you get paid the same as the other sailors.

Let's say, though, that you know you need to make €50,000 annually from writing. Let's further assume that you will work roughly 240 days a year. That means you have to earn €208 a day. Or €26 an hour for that eight-hour day.

Of course, you may decide you can get by on less than €50,000 a year. Just don't kid yourself that taking five weeks to write a script for a radio documentary at a fee of €800 makes sense. It doesn't. An individual fee of €800 looks great – to an amateur. If you are setting out to make a living, or part of your living, from writing, it looks a lot hairier.

The solution is not to go back to whoever commissions documentaries and suggest they need to up the tariff. In present circumstances, that's not going to happen. But even if it did, it's the wrong place to start. The right way to start, when you are setting out to make a living in the business of writing, is to budget your time, so that if you know you will get €200 for a feature, you do not spend three days researching it. You simply can't afford to.

In the beginning, you may be paid less than you want to be paid. Regard the loss as an investment in your future but keep notes of everything you earn. The NUJ will need proof of what you're earning before they'll consider your membership application. Membership of the NUJ is less important than it used to be. Years ago, it was simply impossible to survive as a freelance without NUJ membership. These days, it's possible, but as a life-long member of the NUJ, I would recommend membership, if only for the right to attend the extremely cost-effective training courses they provide.

You will also need to keep receipts of any expenditure you make (computer purchase, phone bill, broadband bill, travel) for your accountant to ensure you get all your tax allowances. An accountant or tax adviser is a wonderful professional who makes sure you get to keep as much money as legally possible out of what you earn. But they also make sure you pay the government the taxes you should pay them, which prevents hassle with the Revenue Commissioners, and history has yet to record an instance of a writer who got into contention with the Revenue Commissioners and won. Conor Cruise O'Brien fought with them in his latter years, claiming that everything he wrote was a tax-exempt work of art. Even if it was a non-fiction book. Even if it was a feature in the *Irish Independent*. The Revenue Commissioners didn't agree with him but he died before the issue was resolved.

You do not need an accountant who has much experience in working with writers. Writers think they're special but in the arithmetic of profit and loss, their work is simple enough to bookkeep for and analyse. Every writer needs an accountant or tax expert who is trustworthy, knows their stuff and is determined to keep you solvent if not profitable.

Ask those of your friends who have small businesses or who work as freelances who they use, because one of the big partnerships, like KPMG, could not put their services at your disposal at a fee that would make sense – at least until you have published your second international bestseller.

I found my tax expert, Darragh O'Shaughnessy, who is now a partner with KSI, before he was qualified. He went to school with my son. Years later, he took over the mad confusion of my money-management and made sense of it. He does have a disconcerting habit, when I ask him a question, of raising one eyebrow and looking at me in total silence for thirty seconds. I never know whether this is because he is impressed by the subtlety of the question or flummoxed by its idiocy.

Even if you are barely out of your teens, talk to your accountant or tax consultant about your pension and start contributing to it now. Small payments over a long period of time become, not just painless, but invisible. You forget you are making them until the great day when you learn you are worth a lot more than you bargained for.

In addition, talk to your accountant or tax expert or business manager about insurance. You never know the day nor the hour that you'll fall off a ladder or develop some illness that will remove your capacity to write, at least for a while. If you were in a small business, the kind of insurance your company should be taking out on you is called (in a sexist way) key man insurance. It protects the company against disaster in the event that their key salesperson (for example) uncaringly pops their clogs or walks into a wind-turbine. It is possible for a sole trader to insure themselves against loss of earnings due to illness or accident and this is worth a little thought at the beginning of your writing career.

5

Freelance Journalism

*...In the current raucously competitive climate, I
doubt I'd make it as a newspaper columnist, since
most now seem to possess unshakeable social and
political convictions and are encouraged to display
them. As for talk radio, I couldn't for the life of
me accommodate all those calls for retribution
and torrents of righteous anger. The demand for
vengeance truly upsets me. What about mercy?*

Deirdre Purcell

To be a freelance journalist means you are your own man or
woman, beholden to nobody, free to work when you want
and laze around when you want, albeit at the expense of sick
pay, compassionate leave, parental leave, stress leave and
a pension. How you view freelance journalism depends on
where you stand. If you want to write serious fiction or non-
fiction but have to keep the bank manager at bay until you
get the first big advance from your publisher, then, inevitably,
you will see freelance journalism as stopgap slumming. If you
yearn for a permanent and pensionable job as an investigative
reporter for a national newspaper or a colour writer for a

Sunday publication, you will see freelancing as a place or state of Purgatory where you have to languish until some editor spots your brilliance and realises they cannot do without having you on staff. If you have confidence in your own speed and flexibility and prefer to work from home rather than trek into an office every day, you will regard freelancing as a tough but enjoyable way to make a living.

It's tough because it comes without safety nets. When, a while back, Joe Duffy was crushed by a reversing car, he was in agony but at least he did not have the added complication of having no salary coming in. He could go through hospital treatment and recovery while someone else filled in for him. This is not the case if you are a freelance. Freelances operate outside the law, in the sense that nobody has much of a duty of care to them, nobody has to provide for them when bad things happen to them, and they can work all the hours God sends without a health and safety officer telling them to go home. (This is mostly because they are already at home, working in the bed or at the desk belonging to the eldest child after the eldest child has gone to bed.)

Freelancing requires a particular breed of person. Typically, freelances are well-read, well-organised, promiscuous in their interests, good at getting along with people and, above all, good at managing their time. However, even if you can demonstrate all these traits, the reality is that, since the recession of 2008 struck, the market for freelance journalism has undergone a violent contraction – although not all that contraction stems from the recession.

The American Journalism Review announced in 2009 that roughly 15 per cent of newsroom jobs in the newspapers in the United States had disappeared during the previous year. Some of this contraction was due to the reduction in advertising income, but some was due to the migration of readers to the internet, rather than to the economic disaster caused by Lehman Brothers and Mr Madoff. All over the world, newspapers are in trouble. Many large and respected papers have folded and the prediction is that many more will close in the next couple of years. Those still in business, especially in Ireland, have been brought almost to their knees by the loss of the substantial income stream represented by the property supplements, now abandoned or etiolated in response to the calcification of the property market and the recruitment pages. In consequence, the freelance market has contracted. Whereas in the past, newspapers tended to carry large numbers of freelances who were so regular in their output and presence as to be virtually indistinguishable from staff members, now the picture is of smaller staffs and fewer freelances.

The freelances who work to the news desks in any of our national papers tend to be freelance only in relation to these outlets. They are sometimes either on staff in a provincial paper or radio station, or have a regular gig (like reporting the local authority meetings) for one or both. Ger Colleran, editor of the Irish *Star,* says:

> Freelances are a very extensive part of our business. Freelance reporters and photographers, particularly. Some of them are local journalists. They realise that what they're working on could have wider application so they present themselves to us; they get on to the news desk. We use them and eventually they become our people in Waterford,

Cork, Limerick, in all parts of the country, over-lapping each other, sending us stories every day. A lot of them spring from stories that appear in local newspapers but which should be liberated for national consideration.

Editors like Colleran regard the news sections of their papers as Open Sesame to anybody who comes along with a good story or photograph, talks to the news editor or the picture editor and begins a relationship of regular supply. The newspaper gains copy without commitment – to them, a freelance is an asset who never becomes a liability, because they're paid for what they produce, rather than for pitching up at the office every day. The tabloid newspapers would be somewhat different from the broadsheets in this area. Broadsheets tend to prefer to have their big news stories written by staff members, although this is changing a bit in the face of incoming contributions from 'citizen journalists'.

The *Mail* group also uses freelances. The Irish *Mail on Sunday* uses more per edition than the *Daily Mail*, according to its editor, Sebastian Hamilton. He adds:

But the *Mail* does have six editions per week. So overall I'd say it balances out. In general, the daily for breaking local news; the Sunday for mega scoops. In terms of finding them, we tend to go geographically: a story breaks in Sligo, the cry goes up: 'Who do we have in Sligo? Who can get to Sligo?' So make sure the desk has all your contact details – and be contactable on them! In terms of them finding us, what they should do is call the news desk and ask to speak to the deputy news editor; have a piece of copy ready and then send it in with lots of contact details. And be ready to answer queries up until late that night. Make friends with the news desk secretary: they can tell you who's in, who's out, who's the best person to talk to…and they ensure you get paid.

The odds may be against a freelance digging up what Hamilton calls a 'mega scoop'. But there's always the chance that you may be lucky – or unlucky – enough to find yourself at the centre of an emerging news story, and in that situation, your mere geographical presence makes you valuable to a newspaper.

For example, one of the most valuable pieces of film, ever, was the tiny segment of 8-mm home movie shot by Abraham Zapruder as the motorcade carrying John F. Kennedy and his wife Jacqueline progressed through Dallas, Texas, in November 1963, to the point where it was fired on by the assassin who killed the President. Zapruder's amateur movie-making – the nearest we have to a complete record of the Kennedy assassination – went around the world and is still used, having made a fortune for the camera-holder's estate.

If you happen to be involved in a disaster, act of war or other news event, how well you do out of it depends entirely on how quickly you can get the story to the best-paying outlet. I was in a taxi passing the Old Bailey when someone blew it up in 1973, which was of no use to me because it was before the days of mobile phones, so by the time I got to where I could use a landline, the wire services were already all over the story. I was in Nassau Street, Dublin, parking my car, when a bomb went off further up the street in what became known as Bloody Friday in May 1974. I rushed to where the explosion had happened, then drove to Middle Abbey Street, where the headquarters of Independent Newspapers was to be found back then, and wrote the story in the newsroom, listening to reporters shouting at each other that another bomb had gone off in Talbot Street, where I knew the man in my life was at the time. (At it turned out, he was uninjured. And unafraid, having worked for years in the North during the Troubles.)

Finally, I was on a flight from the US where the pilot woke the passengers up about an hour away from Ireland to tell us that the cockpit was on fire, that he was bringing the plane to within a thousand feet of the Atlantic to see if they could vent the smoke (in order, we assumed, to see their instruments) and that we must obey the instructions of the cabin crew while they attempted to make Shannon. Make Shannon we did, and the following day I did a twenty-five minute report to Pat Kenny on his morning radio show.

It's wonderful when you find yourself, unexpectedly, the only writer or broadcaster capable of telling a breaking news story but it's nearly as rare as winning the lottery. Your chances of making a living out of freelance journalism are a lot better if you concentrate on the features' pages rather than aim for the news pages, although, even in this area, variations surface between newspapers.

'People trying to get into features would have a much better chance going to, say, *The Irish Times* than coming to us,' says Ger Colleran, editor of the Irish *Star*. 'We have in-house features' staff and maybe one freelance on a constant basis. So our need for freelance feature writers is small.'

The minute he says this, he moderates it, wary of demotivating a writer who is talented but not interested in freelance news reporting. 'A writer who is good and who sticks at it, there's always opportunity for them. They need creativity, though, and they have to be able to do everything.'

In the past, the copy produced by any writer, whether staff or freelance, was mediated (that's a positive word for 'interfered with') by sub-editors, section editors, typesetters and printers, so that it went through a series of processes before it ended up in the printed product.

'The way newspapers are constructed now, there isn't a bank of people waiting to get the raw material in and to turn it into publishable features,' says Claire Grady, Executive Editor of the *Evening Herald*. 'They don't exist any more. Or if they do, they're a dying breed and they're on their way to being completely gone. So a lot of the time, what someone submits in an email is pretty much what goes in.'

Of course, any incoming article gets formatted and somebody puts a headline on it and perhaps a couple of sub-heads through it, but in many newspapers now, there's a pretty good chance that what the writer submits is more or less what the reader will see when they open their newspaper.

'We've cut out all the middle men and middle women, thanks to technology,' says Colleran. This means, in every area of media, that the 'rewrite man (or woman)' is as extinct as the telex. The rewriter was the seasoned old hack who would take disorganised illogical and misspelled material from a journalist and turn it into a coherent and compelling story. It was the norm until twenty years ago and still figured in the newspaper backrooms until relatively recently.

Claire Grady says:

I know from seven years on the news desk of the *Irish Independent*, and it was great experience, that you could have reporters who would be on the radio commentating on topics, giving insights into this, that and the other, who would have great contacts and get the information but my God, they couldn't write to save their lives so it was someone else's job to make sense of what they'd found out.

A groan would go up in the newsroom when sub-editors (because it was usually a sub who ended up rewriting someone's copy) found out that a story was emerging in one geographical area or involving one particular area of expertise, because the newsroom staff knew that the reporter in that area or with that expertise would send in work that was going to have to be unmangled at some speed. Newsrooms did it in the past because it was important that the information was coming from someone with the right contacts. But anybody hoping to make their living out of freelance writing can no longer assume that someone will pull together the tangled strands of a poorly constructed story, remove the misprints ('typos' or typographical errors) and kick grammatical shape into it. They have neither the time nor the inclination.

The first time a freelance leaves a typo in their copy which slithers under the wire and appears in the paper, they have hung a cloud over their own future prospects with that newspaper. The first time a freelance's inaccuracy causes the section editor to receive a solicitor's letter threatening dire consequences over the publication of the inaccuracy, they have volunteered for the dunce's cap and the exit door. Because newspapers simply don't have the layers of protection they used to have. Because of the absence of these protective layers, commissioning editors favour freelances who prove, early on, that they grasp the essentials of grammar and know how to spell (as well as how to avoid libel).

'That's what you want,' agrees Claire Grady. 'There are so many free articles on the internet it shows how many people are prepared to work for free. But if you want to be paid for it, what you want is to be accurate, be reliable and be able to write well.'

Not only have newspapers cut away many of their traditional organisational layers but the old barriers between crafts have eroded. Some years ago I used to take my own photographs to go with stories I had written. It doubled the relatively small fee I earned as a 'stringer' for an English newspaper. But this kind of double-jobbing would not have been possible had I been submitting the material to an Irish newspaper. Writing was one person's job. Taking pictures was another's. Never the twain would meet.

That's history, worldwide. *The New York Times*, last year, looking at the curriculum changes in the Walter Cronkite School of Journalism and Mass Communication on the Phoenix campus of Arizona State University, indicated that the future lay in the hands of 'all-platform journalists', who 'should be able to shoot a video, narrate an audio clip and put up a website as well as write an article and blog about it.'

If you are a writer and plan to make a living, at least in the short term, by freelancing, then you need to be an 'all-platform journalist'. You need a camera (15 mega-pixels) a broadcast quality audio disc recorder, and a smartphone (iPhone or BlackBerry) that will allow you to write copy and transmit it when you do not have your laptop with you. And you need to be speedily competent on all of them. While a features' editor or the editor of a magazine may, this year, take a feature from you and be happy to send out a photographer to get shots of the person you interviewed or the car you test-drove, this is not likely to be the case next year. Turnaround time is getting shorter with every passing week. The story which arrives complete with its own pictures can be processed and in print within hours, whereas the story that requires a separate picture shoot might take a day or days longer to assemble. The key thing the freelance 'all-platform journalist' needs to remember is that selling stories is just the beginning. Solving the editor's problems is the key task, long term.

Sometimes you get lucky. When I was a teenager, working as a researcher on an RTÉ radio programme, one of the frequent guests was Mary Kenny, then the editor of a large section of a national newspaper, now defunct, called the *Irish Press*. One evening, as she left the studio, she instructed me to telephone her the next day. I did. She offered me a freelance job as her fashion and beauty correspondent.

I gazed at myself in a mirror over the telephone. Twenty-five kilos overweight, dressed in clothes that ached for a home in the charity bin in a supermarket car park and as innocent of designer data as an Aborigine accosted in mid-walkabout.

'Mary, I'd love the job and I could do with the money,' I said timidly. 'But I don't know anything about fashion. Or beauty.'

'No problem,' came the reply. 'I don't need you to know anything. I need you to be funny.'

Her position was that she had to have regular features on fashion and beauty because they were mainstays of the features' pages and women's magazines, but at the time, such coverage tended to be somewhat dull, dutifully passing on, as if from a visiting archangel, the word from *Woman's Wear Daily* about what colour would be in vogue eighteen months from now and which fabrics would be popular then. The coverage was cliché-ridden and to some extent still is. I doubt if any single year has gone by since the first year I served as a fashion writer in which the newspaper report of some collection has not borne the headline 'The Long and the Short of It' in reference to hem lengths.

Beauty features were often little more than filler text around a shot of a pretty face, with a few eternal verities from the fashion industry thrown in, chief of those verities being 'cleanse, tone and moisturise.' (These days, 'exfoliate' would be in there somewhere too.)

That first gig was the best fun in the world. I was like a fat version of Anne Hathaway in *The Devil Wears Prada*, hanging around the divas of the fashion and beauty business and getting to go to Paris for the spring collections, with the added bonus that I was permitted to send the whole thing up. It happened because Ireland is small and once a producer or an editor spots someone in one context, they are more likely to think of them when they need a space in a page filled or a package done for, say, a radio programme.

Much harder is the business of cold-calling, where you have to telephone or email a complete stranger in a position of power to interest them in using your work – although you would be surprised by how open many editors are to such calls. Peter Murtagh, Managing Editor of *The Irish Times*, is credited by several columnists on that paper as having spotted and fostered them when they were freelances. Now in charge of the op-ed page (meaning Opposite the Editorial, which denotes, in *The Irish Times* case, the page filled with comment on the stories of the day or the week), he has been surprised in recent years by how much individual prospective contributors have been outnumbered by politicians, businesspeople and academics, not approaching the paper directly but through PR consultancies. He shrugs:

> A lazy editor in my position could become the conduit for every PR company in town. It got so bad in the last two years, every five minutes I'd get a phone call – 'Hello, this is Christine here from Bloggs PR. I just sent an email. Did you get it?' There were so many of them, representing medium-sized companies, semi-state companies and academics, I found myself wondering: when did this happen? PR people ringing on behalf of Professor Somebody, the international expert in quantum physics, who has written a piece? When did people like that start going to PR agencies? Why don't they just send their piece in themselves? More than ever before PR companies are battering at the door trying to get material in.

The fact that such companies are active (if not hyper-active) on behalf of their clients should not put any individual writer off submitting material for the op-ed page in *The Irish Times* (the email address is Opinion@irishtimes.com) or any other daily newspaper.

'It's not a closed circle,' Peter Murtagh confirms. 'Any submission needs to be contemporary, analytical, reasoned. We're looking for well-argued points of view. Punchily written opinion, if possible. Something that's engaging and will grab the reader.'

If the editor of the section is interested but has not encountered the writer up to that point, they will want to telephone to verify who you are, so make sure your numbers are included in the submission.

This contact is necessary to ensure that the writer is who they claim to be and also because the editor may want to query some of the data included in the feature or indicate possible edits. They may also enquire how the writer wants to be described at the end of the published piece or where they can access a good photograph of them.

The editor of every section in every newspaper hates no-hopers who approach them in a ham-fisted, unplanned way, then stalk them to nag about why their piece hasn't appeared. One business editor told me:

> They don't bother first of all to find out the style of the paper. They send me precisely the kind of piece I print once a week from my staff markets expert. What's the point of that? Some of them seem to think that, from a standing start, they're going to do better than someone who has been doing it for years, quite apart from the fact that this man or woman is a staff member. Even if the incoming copy was astonishingly better than their piece is, I'm not in a position to fire them for the benefit of a stranger.

The first step to having a feature accepted by any publication is to work out what that publication is interested in and what style and length are best for it. Sending lengthy upmarket pieces of writing to a sex-obsessed tabloid makes no sense but people do it all the time. I once edited a glossy magazine for teenagers, which, in the way of glossy teen mags, was all about fashion, rock music and how to improve (or initiate) one's sex life.

Every day, I would receive solemn travel features ('The Rose-Red City Half as Old as Time'), articles on simplifying housework ('Burned-on material in a ceramic saucepan may be readily removed using a paste made up of equal parts…') and items on surviving the trauma of advancing years ('Just because your partner has retired doesn't mean you have, too.') What I needed were features on sexually transmitted diseases, quizzes designed to help readers establish their relative levels of cool, smart profiles of newcomers issuing their songs from their garages and snippets of street smarts.

Back then, I had the time to send little notes on the standard rejection slip, indicating how the writer might improve their chances of publication. Now, very few editors have that time, so wannabe contributors sometimes get no response at all, or if they do, it can be a blunt, unevidenced rejection.

According to Sebastian Hamilton of the Irish *Mail on Sunday*, it's a basic rule to:

> …read the paper you're pitching to. We get so many pitches from people who clearly don't have a clue what stories we do, what sections we have. There is no point pitching a business story at us – we don't have a business section. Or a travel feature to the *Daily*. Or some piece of commentary on international affairs. You need to know exactly the

slot you're pitching for: and if it's a feature slot, you need to know how that slot works, what their style is, what length they tend to run to, what kind of pictures they use etc. You also need to find out who runs that section and try and talk to them directly. People who pitch stories at us without having read the paper and knowing how it works are immediately struck off my list of potential people to work for us.

Sebastian Hamilton may sound harsh, but the reality is that wasting an editor's time with an inappropriate offering crafted in ignorance of what he or she is likely to use amounts to insulting that editor to no purpose. Why should they permit you to have a second go?

Once you are established, selling becomes simple. Well, simpler. You know an editor. You ring her. You suggest an idea. She gives the nod, perhaps with a twist, and you get cracking. Or she says she doesn't need that, right now, in which case you get out of her hair immediately.

Before you become established, however, the task is much harder. You first of all find out precisely what name (spell it right) and title your target person owns and fire off a draft feature to them, having made sure they also own the area within which you want to be published. Then ring that person. And only that person. According to Sebastian Hamilton, the worst error a freelance can make is to insist on talking to the news editor – or even worse – to the editor of the daily paper, because they are really busy.

His advice is to talk to someone lower down who has more time. If it's important, they will bring it to the attention of the news editor/editor. Another infuriating error is telephoning moments before the paper's news conference.

'You should find out what time the news conference is on and unless it's mega-urgent, don't call for a good half-hour beforehand, ideally a bit more,' is Hamilton's advice.

Moving speedily on to another feature is a good professional discipline. It may also prevent you from going through the amateur's cycle of paranoia. This is where the writer sends off a feature to a newspaper, has it rejected, and that same evening sees a similar feature in the same newspaper and becomes convinced that they stole the writer's idea.

Paranoia is always pointless but in freelance journalism, is stupidly pointless. The world holds a limited number of ideas, and at any given time, an extremely limited number of topics are newsworthy. Therefore, if a writer crafts a piece about how barter is coming back into style, the chances are that a feature on barter was already in the works and that when it appears, it is coincidental, rather than stolen.

A woman on a Basics of Journalism course I ran a couple of years ago got blind with rage in the classroom over an incident of – as she saw it – a magazine stealing her idea. It had happened towards the end of the previous year, she told the class. She had got a one-line rejection from the editor, saying the feature she had sent was unsuitable – only to discover, the following week, when she bought the magazine, a feature covering the same ground. Everybody in the class was horrified.

The feature was about choosing Christmas toys for toddlers, and my student had submitted it to the magazine on 23 November. The issue of the magazine carrying the similar article appeared on 3 December, although she was able to purchase it a couple of days earlier – most magazines hit the shelves slightly before their official publication date.

It added up to a scenario of theft and pillage as far as the rejected writer was concerned and she was all for taking the publication to the Supreme Court immediately if not sooner. A little investigation knocked the struts out from under her case. The lead time of this particular magazine was eight weeks: in other words, from the time the editorial material was accepted to the time the magazine hit the news stands was eight weeks, during which time design, printing, binding and dispatch (from the Spanish printers to Ireland) happened. So the issue she had bought in the first week in December had actually 'gone to bed' early in October. By the time my trainee submitted her feature, it was, of course, unsuitable because the right time had passed and the need had been met by someone else who had provided the feature two months earlier.

No writer should waste their time developing conspiracy theories about publishers nicking their ideas. And, while I'm at it, another piece of related advice: never append the copyright icon © to your material. It insults the integrity of the editor to whom you end it and marks you out as a gormless amateur.

Another way to insult the recipient and establish yourself as an amateur is to misspell their name. When writers submitting material to me sent it to Terri Prone, it made me wonder about the quality of research that had gone into the writing. (This was before an English publisher decided that renaming me as Terri would double the sales of my novels. It didn't.) The only experience more deflating than being misspelled is receiving material submitted to your predecessor. Particularly if you took over their job ten years ago and they are now eight years dead. The logical inference to be drawn by an editor from this type of carelessness is that you do not read their publication very closely. What is certain is that you are not setting out to solve their problems, which is what a freelance must always be doing.

Establishing yourself as a problem-solving professional means, first of all, sending your stuff to the right person at the right time in the right form. (I'm constantly amazed when an editor on, say, the features' pages of a newspaper gets something that would obviously be more at home on the business pages and takes the trouble to pass it on to the business editor when they could more easily spike it and forget it.)

In addition to sending the piece to the right person, make sure you check the word count on the features they run. If they never go above 650 words, sending them two thousand is daft. But, in addition to sending the right kind of material, you have to prove, at least in the beginning, that you are the right kind of person.

Claire Grady of the *Evening Herald* has a number of rules she apologetically describes as 'glib,' which are, in fact, essential for freelance success:

'Become an expert,' she says. 'Become famous. And no matter who you are, learn to write well. It's difficult for someone to start as a freelance. If I want someone's opinion, I can get loads of opinion on the internet, but if I'm going to put something in my paper, I need to know there is something behind it.'

If Claire Grady is going to take a piece from you arising from the fact that a bridge has collapsed, killing three hundred people, in Manhattan, she needs to know you're a structural engineer who produced a thesis on bridge-building while you were in college, or that, before you settled down, you roamed the world, working in construction and specialising in the building of suspension bridges. The area of expertise does not have to be abstruse. The writer might be an expert on rearing five kids on €200 a week.

'If you want to be a writer, you need to know stuff, not just have opinions on stuff. I might commission an eighteen-year-old to write a piece on what it's like to get the Leaving Cert results, but I really don't want an eighteen-year-old's opinion on what the government should do about the price of oil or about supermarket competition.'

Many people who come to freelance journalism after having had a quite different career tend to undervalue what they know as the result of that earlier career. The old saw, still valid, is, 'Write what you know'.

Since we live in the age of celebrity, it's important to become famous or at least known for having a particular area of expertise. In the beginning, you can write about that, but if you can write, you can then move on to writing about other things, as Claire Grady points out:

> There's a lot of former retired sportsmen who make very good money commentating, either on TV or in the newspapers. People like Eric Miller and Paul Curran. People who are well-known in their particular sport and because they can write and are interested in it, they can go on to have another career. There are people, I'm sure, who were working in finance who could start by writing about their narrow area of expertise. Once they can show they can write, they'll be able to widen the

span of what they write about. It's all about being able to write, being able to think and do it fairly quickly. Once you can do all three, the doors will open up.

Features' editors tend to have a prejudice in favour of matching ages with topics, so, while it's possible for a seventy year old to write about the joys of Victoria Beckham-style five-inch heels, it's a task more likely to be given to someone in their early twenties. Commissioning editors would rather have someone who has kids writing about the cost of school uniforms than to give the job to someone who knows the facts but has no personal involvement. They are always looking for the sense that people know what they're talking about.

Which means that a point of access into mainstream media is a period spent writing for a specialist journal or website, whether it relates to the grocery business, green technologies or health administration. Someone working for such an outlet can easily make the transition into writing about the same topic for a national newspaper.

The editor on the national newspaper must have seen samples of your work (send them or send a link) and have your contact details, so that when some news angle emerges creating the need for a piece with your area of expertise running through it, they can easily make contact with you. In this instance, your credentials and credibility come before personal fame, although they may still want to mention your day job (which is likely to please your main employer no end).

While we're on the subject of famous names, let's lay two ghosts. The first is that you can't make it into journalism if you don't know anybody in the media; that by failing to pick media parents, you may have dealt your potential career a killer blow. Nonsense. It's not who you know that matters, despite all the bitter-loser comments you hear. What matters is who you get to know and how you solve their problem. Gather postal and email addresses as obsessively as you collect mobile phone numbers and constantly update your address books. An editor greeted by name because that detail appears on the screen of your phone immediately gets a sense of your efficiency.

The other issue is writing under a pseudonym, which used to be easy and profitable. I first got into pseudonymous writing when a new editor arrived on a publication to which I supplied two columns a week. He summoned me and indicated he was a force to be reckoned with and that the lamentable standards regnant under his predecessor were no more. It was not quite clear which standards these were, but it sounded as if I, in some way, personified them. I listened to him warbling macho bull for twenty minutes before deciding he was going to be a pain in the arse to work for. It was at this point I told him to stick his columns and left.

Of course, by the time I was half-way home, I realised that this was not necessarily an economically wise step to have taken, so when I got into the house, I changed the typeface, layout and margins on my computer, dashed off a column and sent it to him from my sister's address under a false name. He accepted it and ran it straight away, demanding more along the same lines and – maddeningly – paying me more for not being me than he had paid me for being me. He did occasionally issue invitations to come and meet him face to face, but I gave him the impression, whenever such an invite issued, that I was particularly busy at that time and the longing went off him. He never discovered who I was. The system worked so well that I eventually operated under eleven different aliases, and once filled an entire page of *The Irish Times* with three related features, each written under a different pseudonym. The features' editor on the paper of record knew who was behind each of the names and was happy to grant me cover. (At the same time, the late, wonderful David Marcus, without being in the know, was publishing my short stories in the *Irish Press* under a pseudonym made up of the names of my two nephews.)

That could never happen, these days, because, as Claire Grady explains, of the need to have a photograph of the writer incorporated into any opinion piece:

> The trend in every newspaper is to want a face to go with the piece, because we have become so visual. So we're not comfortable with people writing under pen names. If you're giving your opinion, we need your credentials and you have to be able to put your name over it so that readers can say, 'Oh, I know this writer, they're right-wing or left-wing, I read them before. I like the way she talks, or I think he doesn't know what he's talking about.' You want to build up the relationship, and to do that, the reader has to be able to see your photograph and know what you look like.

Very occasionally, of course, the individual in the photograph and the actual writer of the piece are not one and the same. Now and again, a newspaper will take a punt on someone who is the flavour of the month and hire them. The fact that they may not be able to write, or may not have the time to write, is beside the point. The newspaper will appoint someone to telephone the ostensible author, get some ideas from them, then craft a feature in what becomes the style of the person whose name and fame are being purchased.

Other than that, the only occasion on which a pseudonym may be used is to protect a victim. If, for example, an horrific rape case goes through the courts and the victim is willing to write about the experience, a newspaper may accept their piece and print it under a false name or no name, in order to protect their anonymity. But this kind of situation is exceedingly rare.

For the features' pages of newspapers, forget about using a pseudonym unless you are household-name famous. Until that day comes, they will want your name and face on anything you write. Which can cause problems for a penurious freelance. Because, although a particular newspaper may not pay you enough to live on, they are likely to get stroppy if they see your work appearing in other places because it disturbs the integrity of their brand.

The only way around this is to be an all-platform journalist. Newspapers may get shirty about you appearing in another newspaper but may be quite pleased to have you participate in radio programmes, particularly if you are introduced as being their columnist. Similarly, they may have no problem seeing you on a reality TV programme or appearing in a blog. They just don't want to share your name with some other entity in the same business and probably competing with them.

Before you get to the stage where a newspaper becomes possessive about you, you have to get qualified, (as in becoming expert on some topic), get famous, (to a degree) write well and get in touch with the commissioning editor. They'll usually take a phone call unless it's from a regular torment. Ring to find out who's commissioning pieces and their email address. Then send them a note about the subject you'd be interested in covering. Either give them a flavour of how you'd tackle it and some indication of other stuff you've written or submit the piece already written.

At this point, you get to walk the fine line between promoting and pestering. You can ring the commissioning editor to let them know that you have sent them a piece on the new plastic guns that are fooling airport security scanners, but you must make it clear that the only reason you're ringing them is because it's so topical and you wanted to alert them that it should be in their inbox. Don't ask them if they are going to use it or not going to use it. Just make sure they know where to reach you, if/when they want to reach you, and get off the line. They're busy. They're hassled. And they're not in the business of therapy.

Once you've sold a feature, you must deliver. No excuse for failure is acceptable to a hassled editor. They've set aside space in their paper for a piece they expect by a particular time. They expect it to be proofread, accurate and clean. They expect you to draw their attention to any possible legal problems implicit in an aspect of the piece. They don't care if your dog gets run over, your electricity fails, your computer freezes, you get a migraine or your car has a knock in its engine. They're not inhuman, but, from where they stand, dog, ESB, PC, sore head and car noises are your problems. If you've agreed to deliver, deliver. If you know you can't deliver, either become unobtainable or tell them you'd love to but can't.

Never share your private miseries – they may remember

them and feel inhibited about ringing you the next time. Worse, they may not remember them, but retain an overall impression of you as that freelance with the complicated home-life. To be seen as someone with a complicated home-life is detrimental to career progress in many sectors, but it is frankly lethal in freelance journalism. Even if you're standing in the kitchen barefoot in a slippery morass of broken glass and olive oil, clutching a croupy baby in one hand and the divorce papers in another with the other phone ringing and the kitchen curtains going up in flames, you must sound, to a commissioning editor, as if you were calmly in charge of the world. Why? Because freelance journalism is the definitive no-excuses business.

What it has in common with all businesses, however, is a human dynamic. I once heard my husband on the phone to someone in RTÉ he clearly was on good terms with. The two of them exchanged jokes, he gave the man on the other end of the line some information, and the encounter ended happily for all parties.

'Who was that?' I asked, and Tom named the man. The name meant nothing to me.

'Guy at the security kiosk,' Tom explained.

I laughed. 'Not somebody important, like the Director General?'

'Much more important to know the guy in security by his first name than know the DG by his,' Tom responded, as if it was obvious.

It's not obvious and many freelances miss it. They are brusque with whoever answers the phone in the media outlet they have called if that person isn't the editor or producer they're used to. Big mistake. Huge. It's a mistake, first of all, in simple human respect. But it's also a career mistake. Too many people create today's network, never notice when it becomes yesterday's network and make no effort to create tomorrow's network. Be pleasant to everybody around the editor or producer to whom you work and get to know them. It'll be more fun in the present and, in the future, they may become the person you're reporting to, so it helps if you don't treat them like dirt when they're low on the ladder.

Freelancing is not a mysterious, closed trade. Indeed, according to Sebastian Hamilton, editor of the Irish *Mail on Sunday*, the single most important factor in successful freelance journalism – or any form of journalism – is the simple willingness to work hard. He admits:

> This may involve missing out on movies, nights in the pub, weekends, gigs, footy matches, quality time with your other half. But it's the big determinant of success. If you're not up for that – for dropping everything on a rain-sodden night to go and doorstep someone – then really you should look for a job in an office where you get a nice name-tag and finish at 5pm. If you do want to be a journalist, then the harder you work, the luckier – and richer – you'll get.

6

Writing Features

There is not much to be said for the recommendation, so often heard, to serve an apprenticeship to journalism if you intend to write fiction.

But a journalist's career does teach two lessons which every writer needs to learn –

That it is possible to write for long periods without fatigue, and that if one pushes on past the first weariness one finds a reservoir of unexpected energy – one reaches the famous 'second wind'.

Dorothea Brande, *Becoming a Writer*

Features come in all sorts of shapes and sizes. In theory, they all belong to the same species, but in practice, they can be amazingly different from one another. The following are ten examples of the types of material crossing the desk of a features' editor:

1. A five-part series, each component section of which is three thousand words long, investigating healthcare

systems world wide, and requiring the writer to travel to four overseas countries and interview several ministers for health while travelling

2. A half-page excursion into green goods for the home, broken up into small paragraphs, each topped by a photograph, showing items like iron frames for squashing wet paper into homemade briquettes and gadgets on pulleys allowing the drying of clothes in front of a stove

3. An impassioned plea by a recently-published novelist for the reintroduction of Bible classes in schools

4. An attack on a government minister by the opposition spokesperson with the same portfolio

5. A three-hundred word explanation for the previous night's three-hour collapse of Google

6. A funny exploration of a recent study into the relative intelligence of golden retrievers and black crows

7. An archaeologist's account of a dig on a city dump and what it revealed about city-dwellers over the past ten years

8. A two-hundred-word regular piece on the significance of first names.

9. A response to a reader's question about job interview preparation.

10. A Q&A with a celeb

Now, let's look at how each of these features happens and how the writers of the features may be chosen.

1. *A five-part series, each component section of which is three thousand words long, investigating healthcare systems world wide, and requiring the writer to travel to four overseas countries and interview several ministers for health while travelling*

This is the kind of feature series commissioned only by a major broadsheet, like the *Sunday Business Post* or *The Irish Times*. Typically, the writer is an indentured freelance, someone in their thirties or forties with a long-established expertise in a specialist area who is happy to belong to one newspaper without being on staff.

An editor commissioning such a series will take some time before making the decision to allocate the level of funding it requires and will do so only when they are absolutely sure that the chosen writer will deliver. It rarely happens that a newcomer to journalism wins such a gig, even if they are knee-deep in specialist knowledge, because editors may have concerns that the expert will not be able to make their data interesting to outsiders.

Any writer who is commissioned to undertake such a task should do a little lateral thinking. Does it have peripheral possibilities? If the interviews were recorded, could they give rise to a radio documentary? Or a book? Most newspapers are happy enough to see such secondary use of their material, as long as they know about any such plans in advance and as long as they get a credit.

2. *A half-page excursion into green goods for the home, broken up into small paragraphs, each topped by a photograph, showing items like iron frames for squashing wet paper into homemade briquettes and gadgets on pulleys allowing the drying of clothes in front of a stove*

This kind of half-page is usually an advertising feature: in other words, the idea may come, not from the editorial side of the newspaper but from the advertising side. In the past, editorial and advertising regarded each other as necessary evils and anybody writing an advertising feature was tainted with commercialism. This view has substantially changed and some fine writers now produce such material all the time. If you're interested in this kind of work, find out who, in the publication, commissions such articles and what rules obtain. (Flexing your ethical muscles by describing as a waste of money a product the makers of which have taken out a large advertisement on the same page may be satisfying to your soul but is likely to shorten your shelf life on pages such as these.)

3. *An impassioned plea by a recently-published novelist for the reintroduction of Bible classes in schools*

This kind of piece is usually part of the marketing duties imposed on novelists. The publicist for the publisher will want to place stories about anything vaguely related to the theme of the new book in as many publications as possible, so that the book and the writer become familiar enough to readers to make them pick up the novel when they spot it in a bookshop.

4. *An attack on a government minister by the opposition spokesperson carrying the same portfolio*

Variations on this kind of feature include an attack on a proposed policy which might damage the prospects of an industrial sector, in which case the feature is written by something from the industry in question or from IBEC (Irish Business and Employers' Federation). The point is that, increasingly, politicians and businesspeople, as well as advocates and activists, need to be able to put their point of view in writing at short notice. Either they take a course and do it themselves or a freelance writer cosies up to them with an offer to undertake the task after being briefed by a fast phone call.

5. *A three-hundred word explanation for the previous night's three-hour collapse of Google*

Consider this scenario. You are a card-carrying computer nerd. You worked out what happened long before anybody else did. At this point, you had a choice. You could stick the insight up on your website or Facebook page, to impress, free, gratis and for nothing, the people who already find you pretty impressive, or send it to a newspaper in the hope of making some money. Forget Facebook. Send it to an editor. Look at it this way – even if the newspaper doesn't use it, they now know they have access to a bright, fast responder who understands viruses and hacking. So, if you go back to them in a week with a feature on how to speed up your computer without installing a new hard disc, they are more likely to consider it than they would have before you responded to the Goggle collapse.

6. *A funny exploration of a recent study into the relative intelligence of golden retrievers and black crows*

Never forget, as a freelance, that certain topics always attract attention. They include: pets, children, mothers, money, sex, boyfriends (attached or unattached to the sex) being too fat, being too thin and other people's driving/bad habits.

Add to that the fact that studies of all kinds, no matter how statistically invalid, fascinate readers. If you trawl the web first thing each morning, you will invariably find a study someone has done on something oddball or a survey recently published about an unexpected theme or topic, like, 'Four out of Ten Sons Get Mothers to Do Their Laundry.' (I made that up, but, sure as eggs, it will turn up somewhere as the outcome of research.)

The survey or study will give you the news peg on which to hang a feature you have already written or on which to base a fresh essay.

7. *An archaeologist's account of a dig on a city dump and what it revealed about city-dwellers over the past ten years*

Everybody's day job has aspects that rivet the uninvolved. Write about them. And if you think nobody with their head screwed on the right way would want to read about vertical sections of excavated garbage, think again. A book on the topic did very nicely, thank you, a few years back.

8. *A two-hundred word regular piece on the significance of first names*

Sadly, this is the kind of regular slot that is disappearing from newspapers. That's not to say that it is disappearing from other media. In fact, this is where you can explore the wonderful possibilities of specialist media. The magazine shelves are full of publications which reach a discrete audience, whether that audience is made up of cigar smokers, new mothers or furniture restorers. While they tend not to pay over-generously, which is a disadvantage, such magazines rarely have a big staff, which is an advantage. Because they don't have a cast of thousands from which to draw, they rely on the contributions of freelances. If you can sell a parenting magazine or a magazine aimed at women planning to have babies the idea of a regular piece about first names, not only will you have a nice little earner in that slot, you can become an expert on names and their importance in human relations, and end up doing occasional (and possibly better paid) inputs into newspapers or radio/TV programmes.

The same applies no matter what your special interest is. Find out all you can about any specialist publication related to that interest and start getting published between its covers. It may be the key to a wider market. A cover letter saying, 'I'm a regular columnist with *Bricklayers Monthly* on the topic of worker-compensation,' provides a comforting concept of you as an expert to a potential employer in mainstream media.

9. *A response to a reader's question about interview preparation*

This is where the man who has become known as the Career Doctor started.

Eoghan McDermott runs the Career Clinic in the Communications Clinic, advising people on how to go about job interviews. The *Sunday Tribune* contacted him and asked if he could do a feature on the topic. He did it (with much trepidation). It ran in the paper. It got response, much of which took the form of questions. The paper decided to run a weekly item responding to readers' queries.

Matt Cooper's *Last Word* programme on Today FM noticed the item and tried Eoghan out in a two-hander about jobs, careers and recruitment. The two-hander became a monthly slot. Between Eoghan's daily work, the *Sunday Tribune* column and his Today FM appearances, it wasn't long before he had enough material to write a book about getting a job in the recession or fixing an ailing career.

In Eoghan's case, the person who had the idea for the *Sunday Tribune* item was Business Development Manager Andrew Mernagh. But you don't have to wait for a commissioning editor to a) dream up a good idea and b) decide you are the person to deliver on it. If you have expertise, suggest the item. You should be warned that if the expertise you will be demonstrating has anything to do with the company employing you, the paper may suggest that a byline mentioning your company name would be a good quid pro quo and that of course you wouldn't expect to be paid on top of getting such a great marketing opportunity in a newspaper which reaches so many hundreds of thousands of your potential customers. If you're new to writing and ultimately want to do more writing than consulting or software engineering, take this deal. It will provide you with regular deadlines and the habit of writing.

10. A Q&A with a Celeb

It happens. Now and again, it happens. Just once in a very blue moon. A writer, or would-be writer, who has never before interviewed anybody famous, gets a chance at it. They and the film star have a mutual friend. Or they just get lucky. Grab the chance with both hands and your teeth. Read Chapters 7 and 8 on conducting the interview and writing the profile. Bring with you the best camera you can borrow.

Apropos the camera, you may find that the celeb has a bank of photographs they would prefer you to use. Especially if you meet them in a private situation where they are neither made up nor dressed up. That's fine. Just make sure you get a photograph of yourself with them. This picture will be a souvenir, but much more than a souvenir. It will serve as evidence that you truly met the person you profile. This matters. Clifford Irving, a respected fiction and non-fiction writer, got a hefty advance ($100,000 back in 1971 was extremely hefty) from prestigious US publisher McGraw Hill to write a biography of the mad reclusive millionaire, Howard Hughes, based on interviews he claimed to have conducted with him. He produced large sections of a manuscript which seemed to have the hallmarks of an international bestseller. McGraw-Hill were persuaded of Hughes's untypical co-operation with the book by Irving's production of letters from the recluse and announced the title in its list of forthcoming books.

The problem was that the letters were forgeries. Irving had never met Howard Hughes and Howard Hughes became sufficiently irate about the prospect of publication of a supposedly 'authorised' biography to make a phone call disavowing Irving, who eventually admitted what he'd done and went to prison for the scam. (On the other hand, it has to be said in his favour that when he emerged from clink, he went on to write several more books, and they were good enough – or perhaps he was notorious enough – for a publisher other than the one he had conned to publish them. One of the books, called *The Hoax*, loosely based on the Howard Hughes episode, went on to become a film – partly written by Irving.)

The ten features listed at the beginning of this chapter do not represent the totality of what appears, on any given day, in newspapers and magazines. They are, however, the kinds of features most likely to be written by freelances. Regular columns are already allocated, and even if you think you could knock the socks off Kevin Myers, Justine McCarthy or John Waters, editors are unlikely to take a punt on an unknown.

Similarly, the regular slot like 'On This Day', where what happened on this particular day a century or half a century ago are recycled, or the 'Quotes of the Week', where someone assembles the most interesting or outrageous comments uttered in the previous seven days, are already in the ownership of another writer, probably a staff member, and casting an envious eye on them is not only a waste of your time, but if articulated to an editor, will define you as hopelessly naive. Concentrate on getting some material published on a topic that you already know a lot about. When you have achieved some reputation as a writer who delivers, editors will begin to commission features from you. On this and on other topics.

Some features are planned months in advance; others are commissioned hours before the paper hits the street. This can lead to confusion on the part of the writer. One morning a few weeks back, the commissioning editor of the *Evening Herald* reached me as I was on my way to Croke Park to give a talk. Could I turn a piece around by 8.30? It was then a quarter to eight and I figured I would be in the Croke Park car park in ten minutes. Yes, I said, I would be delighted. I took the briefing and only then remembered I didn't have my computer with me.

However, I did have my BlackBerry, so, once I reached the car park, I started to hammer the 650 words into the phone. (If any reader knows how to get a word count on a feature out of a BlackBerry, please let me know. I hate having to guess.) By 8.20 the feature was done, dusted and transmitted.

When I came out after the lecture and turned the BlackBerry back on, up popped a message from a radio station inviting me to talk to them at three about 'that feature you wrote'. I texted them to say I would be delighted and shortly after three, their phone call came through and I found myself on the air, talking about the feature. Except the feature they were asking about was one I had written three months earlier, for a magazine that was only now appearing on the news stands. Could I remember the bloody thing? No. But fortunately the interviewer quoted big chunks out of it so all I had to do was react. The curious thing was that, because I had written it so long before, the magazine feature felt like history as far as I was concerned, whereas to the interviewer, it was just as topical as the feature in the evening newspaper.

A propos of interviews arising out of your writing a feature, it may come as a disappointment to you to learn that the writer does not, usually, get paid for secondary coverage arising out of a feature. The radio station that interviews you regards a mention of the publication in which the original piece appeared as sufficient payment.

To survive as a freelance feature writer, you must have a number of customers, some of them paying and some of which use you without paying but help to keep your profile reasonably prominent. A writer should not feel they're home and dry because, say, the features' editor of a national newspaper likes their work. They should also think of areas like weekend reviews (which can usually handle lengthier pieces than daily papers) and the book pages (book reviews do not pay highly but you get the book for free).

A mosaic of markets is always better than one. In fact, having one and only one customer is dangerous. People in media die, just as people in other professions do. People move. People lose their jobs. Just as importantly, people change allegiances. Worst of all, people develop coercive notions of ownership: you're mine, you'll dance when I tell you to dance. No freelance writer should ever be dependent on any single publishing entity for more than 40 per cent of their income, and if the dependence goes above 60 per cent, that's exactly what it is; dependence.

At the beginning of their careers, many feature writers find it difficult to start in first gear. They need to rev on the spot for a while before they get moving. If you're that kind of writer, what you must do is get the feature written, then read it through, asking yourself, 'At what point do I stop revving and get moving?' It may be that this happens after one paragraph. It may take three. But the difference is palpable and the point of take-off unmistakable. Once you have spotted the place where the feature takes off, cut everything that comes before that sentence. Even if you really like it.

Somerset Maugham said that writers should reread their material, find the three things they like best, and cut them out as likely to be self-indulgent or merely decorative. Showing off is not permitted. Every time you set out to write, you should aim to obey another of Maugham's rules. He defined the task of a writer as being to 'make old things new, and new things familiar'.

It sounds simple but dozens of emailed articles arrive

in newspaper offices every day in which solid, worthy, predictable and old points are made in solid, worthy, old and predictable ways. The classic example is the feature about the difference between dog lovers and cat lovers. This argument is five hundred years old and wasn't that riveting the first time it was articulated. It still gets into print because an editor who has just bought a dog or a cat is at just the right stage to find merit in it. Watch out for it. It tends to take the form of a flaccid excursion into unevidenced prejudices.

In addition to making the old new and the new familiar, the freelance feature writer has to do it in the voice of the publication to which they're submitting their material.

Every newspaper, without necessarily stating it, has a list of what it likes and what it does not like. These preferences – or 'values,' if you want to get heavyweight about it – add up to the distinctive 'voice' of the paper. This voice can be divined by anyone paying close attention to the publication. It may take freelance writers a few editions to work out what kind of personalities the paper favours.

One paper, for example, may like a sensible woman who happens to be glamorous as well, so they will constantly feature RTÉ's Miriam O'Callaghan. Another paper may like Jordan up to the point where she is seen as disregarding her kids and her husband and reverting to type. Some papers love victimhood. Some love attacking the system, particularly when the system – whether in the form of the government, the HSE, a local authority or a bank – is seen as coming down hard on the small man or woman. Some hate handouts and regard themselves as the protectors of the decent, diligent, employed reader. To write cogently for a publication, you need to know what the publication's starting position and values are, bearing in mind that they are not often publicly expressed but that an editor who is, of necessity, steeped in them every day, may get impatient with a freelance writer who proposes an op-ed feature which runs so counter to these values that the editor wonders if the writer lives on another planet.

The other factor which frustrates section editors who are willing, nay eager, to publish freelance material is when the writer produces a stellar first offering, an acceptable second offering and a frankly dire third offering. One editor told me:

> You feel the required level of polish is not there, and has not been there since the first piece. A really good piece of writing you don't really have to do anything to. It may not win the Booker, but it's grand. Fit for purpose. It engages me, there's a thread through it that leads me along and there's a nice little bit at the end. You can get people who send in a letter and you accept a piece from them because it's fine, but later pieces don't match that standard and you wonder if they just had that piece in them, or perhaps just one good piece a year. You don't have time to tutor them, though.

That presents an interesting problem for newcomers to the writing game. Editors simply do not have the time to provide tutorials but every writer needs a mentor. It doesn't have to be someone steeped in journalism. As long as the person likes reading and has a low boredom threshold, they'll do. My mother was always a wonderful writer's mentor, although she never in her life published anything, because she was impatient, easily bored, acutely resistant to cliché and regarded any feature that didn't tell her something she didn't already know in a lively funny way as a waste of her time.

When you go looking for a mentor, search for someone who doesn't want to write themselves. Seek out someone who doesn't instantly want to edit your piece. Most people who have come through journalism instinctively reach for a red pen when they are offered someone else's work to read before it's published. Don Hewitt, the key producer of America's *60 Minutes* TV programme, got his comeuppance, on this matter, from one of the best writers in America, Molly Ivins.

It happened after he had marked changes he felt should be made to a commentary she had written for the programme. Ivins fixed him with a filthy look and spoke. 'The strongest human emotion is neither love nor hate,' she told him. 'It is one person's desire to fuck with another person's copy.'

Do not, when selecting your mentor, pick someone who really wants to write the piece for you. Pick someone who wants you to become the best writer you can be and who will be honest about being bored, confused or belittled by something you have written. Someone, in short, who will help to prevent you failing at the second or third fence by producing copy that is insufficiently polished.

Falling at the second fence can, of course, also happen when a writer misses a deadline. Even the *Evening Herald*'s equable Claire Grady gets slatey as to the eyes about that possibility. She says bluntly:

> They fail once, and only once. That sounds very ruthless. But there's a lot of people out there looking for work. OK, maybe that's a bit harsh. I'm

not quite as cruel as that. I usually give people a second chance and I don't just mean me. When people fail, it means they haven't filed on time or what they deliver wasn't what you asked for. If they miss the deadline, you always have a Plan B but Plan B is always inferior to Plan A. If what they deliver wasn't what you wanted, you have to be fair. You have to ask yourself: did you get your brief across so poorly that they got the wrong end of the stick. But if someone simply fails to deliver copy on time, then they'll be lucky if they get another chance.

7

Conducting Interviews

Writing is easy.
  All you do is stare at a blank sheet of paper until
drops of blood form on your forehead.

Gene Fowler

Writers, artists, politicians, musicians, architects, business-people, athletes, broadcasters – they appear every day in newspapers, TV and radio programmes. Being interviewed. Interviews and personality profiles are media staples. They're also a lot of fun to do. Once you know how to do them.

If you know someone who is famous for some reason, think about using them as the subject for a profile interview. You couldn't? Why not? We hate to admit it, but most of us love talking about ourselves, so you would be handing the famous person an opportunity to do just that. Not to mention the fact that people love to be asked for help of any kind. Within your reach is a range of the famous or nearly famous or the eccentric or interesting. You may not know them intimately yourself, but you undoubtedly know someone who does know them. Make a list. Check it twice. Go after the individuals on it. After you have internalised this chapter.

Interviewing is one of the most rewarding areas of media, whether you do it on TV, radio, the web or for publication. You get to meet the famous, the interesting and the odd, discover unknown aspects of their lives, and write about them for money. You have to admit, that's a cool deal.

Interviewing starts with the 'six honest serving men' of Rudyard Kipling's rhyme:

> *I keep six honest serving-men*
> *(They taught me all I know),*
> *Their name are What and Why and When,*
> *And Which and Where and How.*
> *I send them over land and sea*
> *I send them East and West*
> *But after they have worked for me*
> *I give them all a rest...*

Those six serving men are all you need when you are setting out to do an interview. Many novice journalists believe that if they don't have information-laden, deadly impressive questions, they will lose out. Not so. After an interview, what you want, as a writer, are good quotation from the interviewee, not a warm reflection of how wise and witty you were. Never concentrate on show-off questions. Instead, listen to the first answer, and out of that answer, frame the next question, which may simply be:

'Why do you say that?'

or

'When did that happen?'

or

'And then?'

A great question is one which gets the interviewee to be revealing about themselves, not one which sounds good of itself.

Learn to frame open questions. Never make a big long statement that invites a 'Yes' or 'No' response. You hear it all the time on radio:

> It has been said that your company has shown some disregard for the rule of law in relation to its purchases of raw materials over the past few years. It is also clear that your company has ignored many bylaws in the disposal of effluent and that the long-term implications of this are very serious. Are you satisfied with your company record?

The interviewee, in this instance, has had several years in which to formulate a reply. The dread possibility is that it might be a one-word affirmative.

Closed questions often start with 'Do you?' As in, 'Do you feel that murdering babies at random is a poor approach to fighting a war?'

Open questions, in contrast, tend to start with 'How?' As in, 'How do you view murdering babies at random?'

Sometimes, the open question can be quite directive. Gay Byrne, for half a century, held the franchise on this kind of opening salvo:

'Talk to me about...'

'Tell me about...?'

This formula gets the interviewee to provide a big dense answer which allows you to listen carefully and decide which theme will be most productive to pursue.

Listening is key to interviewing. If you listen closely, you hear more than words. You hear sensitivities, boredom, defensiveness. You hear the deadly vocal tune famous people develop when they get launched on their 'legend:' the self-portrait that has become so familiar to them that they can rhyme it off without thought. You don't want legend. If they're used to rhyming it off, readers are used to reading it or hearing it from them and they want something new, something different, something surprising about them. So listen for that speech tune and cut across it.

You can't listen adequately without looking while you listen. We hear with our eyes as well as our ears. It's through watching someone closely that we notice discrepancies between what they're saying and the expression on their face or the way they shift about while saying it. That need to watch as well as listen is where a recording device comes into play. I have such a high anxiety level that whenever I have to do an interview, I bring two separate recording gadgets for fear one of them proves to be a lemon. Whenever I'm about to kick this habit, one of the recorders does prove to be a lemon and reinforces the need for them to travel in couples. You must always announce your intention to use the machine. Recording people without their knowledge is unethical and in some circumstances, illegal. Tell your interviewee you do not have shorthand and don't want to get anything they say wrong, so this is your method of note-taking.

Make sure the batteries are new and that you are familiar with the machine so that you don't waste time at the outset – and make your subject and yourself nervous – by doing a dozen test recordings and getting a poor result. Your interviewee should be flattered by your attention and how fascinating you find them, not filled with doubt as to your overall competence based on a free sample of ineptitude with a digital recorder.

Keep the recording for several weeks after your interview, feature (or book) appears. Once the piece is published, the subject may decide they didn't say what you have quoted them as saying. This can happen because of public reaction to the published material or because of the reactions of families and friends. You need to have the tapes to prove what they did say. Memory is a funny thing: the interviewee may remember the interview quite differently from the recollection of the interviewer and they may not even remember that the interview was recorded. Whether you carry one recorder or two, you still need a clipboard or a writing pad, because you will want to make notes about the subject's demeanour, grooming, clothes and surroundings.

You don't, going into an interview, need to bring a list of questions. Let me put that more forcefully. No interviewer worth a damn ever brings a list of questions into an interview, whether it's on TV or for the next day's paper. Once you have a list of questions, you can't watch and listen freely. You can't spot added value or pick up an inconsistency.

By all means, bring a note of the areas through which you wish to take the interviewee. Not a series of questions. Just a set of areas to remind you of something you might otherwise forget. Make your notes brief and (if you don't handwrite them) feed them out in big print so you can refer to them quickly, without destroying the relationship you are building up with the person you are interviewing. This way, you can concentrate on what you want them to say, rather than on what you want to ask.

Be wary of Googling the person. Internet research is dangerously easy. At a few keystrokes you can learn everything that has ever been written about your subject and everything they have ever said. The danger therein is that you seek to make them repeat the best of what they have already said, and take you through aspects of their life which are already common knowledge. The end result will be recycled, reheated celeb, than which nothing is worse, except perhaps recycled, reheated researcher interviews.

Recycled researcher interviews happen on some TV programmes where a researcher is sent out to get to know Joe Bloggs. They ask Joe Bloggs questions. They observe him. They listen to him. Then they come back to the TV station and transcribe it all. Then they pick out the bits they prefer, and telephone the subject to tell him he will be asked these questions in this order and he must remember to say exactly what they said to the researcher. Then the researcher prepares a brief for the TV interviewer, indicating that if the questions are asked in the set order, the end results will be safely predictable. Then (if the programme has the time for this crap) the TV interviewer goes into studio and interviews the researcher, who parrots what the interviewee will eventually say. This kind of approach is why so many celeb television interviews are so deadly in their predictability.

Be wary of forcing your interviewee into the tunnel of their earlier comments. It stereotypes and insults them. Because Marian Keyes once talked with touching frankness about her alcoholism, almost every subsequent interviewer has decided that the illness is the essence of Marian as a writer. It isn't, wasn't and never will be, yet Marian, when she does the publicity for her latest novel, always finds herself being asked the same tedious questions and – because she is so endlessly obliging – not just answering them but trying desperately to illustrate these answers in some fresh and exciting new way.

This form of lousy interviewing pre-dates the internet. Film star Richard Burton was so bored with it that, at the height of his fame, when a journalist approached him begging for an interview, his answer was terse.

'If you can ask me a question no interviewer has ever asked me before, Ill give you the interview.'

'Are you good in bed?' she asked.

Burton laughed, admitted that nobody had ever asked him that before, and gave her the interview. (She got a book out of it, later, asking a series of famous people the same question.)

Any time an interviewee says, 'I'm always asked that question,' give yourself a smack upside the head. Not that it is the worst possible response. Sometimes, an interviewee can get so irritated by being asked a prepared list of boring questions that they let fly. One interviewer, after half an hour of such questions, made the mistake of asking Alfred Hitchcock what had been the lowest moment in his career.

'I am afraid this is,' came the crisp reply.

However, you can give yourself a pat on the back whenever an interviewee stops dead and tells you that not only have they never been asked that question before, but that they have never thought about the matter raised. If that happens, shut up and let them do their thinking and talking on the spot.

The other great compliment interviewers should cherish is when the interviewee says, 'I don't know why I'm telling you this,' or, 'Nobody but my mother/husband/wife knows this about me.' When this happens, it means they are sharing something they are not used to sharing or exploring something they haven't been forced to examine up to this point.

You don't have to ask an extraordinary or impertinent question, if you want to get the best out of a subject, but you should go to any lengths required to avoid an interview which results in your subject telling you precisely what they've said to dozens of earlier interviewers.

When you get to interview a writer, you should do your best to know their work. (This isn't the same as reading the work of other journalists work about them.) If the writer is on the publicity tour (see Chapter 11) their publicist will send you the book and background material. If you do not have time to read it, the priority areas are the cover blurb, introduction and – if it's non-fiction – the index. The latter will spark off a famous name or an issue – read the relevant bit and you will undoubtedly get a question out of it.

If you don't know a writer and you know you really should, it's time to phone a friend. Every one of us has at least one friend who reads obsessively. Just ring them and ask them a) to give you a flavour of this writer's work and b) to tell you what they would love to learn about the writer.

Before you go to the location where the encounter is to happen, put the interviewee's name, title and organisation or book title on the page in front of you. Blanks happen. Particularly if you're nervous – and most of us get nervous when faced with interviewing a household name.

One final caveat before you start any interview. KYOS. Keep Yourself Off-Stage. You are not the famous person. Your subject is the famous person. Shut up about yourself. Don't tell them about the day you've had, how your mother always loved them (a singularly unwelcome compliment regularly made to older interviewees, since it implies that they're as historic as the faces on Easter Island to anyone as young as you are. Maeve Binchy is sometimes told the interviewer's granny loves her stuff.) Don't say, 'I absolutely agree with you and that matches my own experience.' Who the hell cares?

Occasionally, because not all famous people are self-focussed, they will express interest in the interviewee. Although Carly Simon is believed to have written her hit song, 'You're So Vain', about film star Warren Beatty, any student of celebrity interviews knows that Beatty made every interviewer feel glorious by asking them all about themselves and behaving as if he was genuinely interested. If you meet a Warren Beatty or a George Clooney, who seems to do the same, get over the personal reinforcement, get the focus back on them and get asking questions.

Be clear, before you start an interview, how long you have with the interviewee. Sometimes, you have the space to create a relationship. Sometimes, you have to move more speedily than is comfortable.

Being warm and pleasant does not mean you cannot ask difficult questions. One of the great journalists and lecturers on journalism, Jessica Mitford, taught her students to relax their interviewee before introducing their more contentious questions. Years later, when one of her students applied the lesson in an interview with Mitford herself, all she could do was laugh with rueful admiration.

If you have to ask a difficult question, you do not have to make a major production out of it. Remember, always, that it is the answer that's going to appear in your profile and that is, in consequence, is of prime importance. So if you want to ask a man how he lives with himself after selling his daughter into slavery, there's no point in making a command performance out of it. Shout a reproachful accusation at the man and he may walk out. Ask the very same question with wondering gentleness, and you are likely to get a super – and eminently usable – answer.

Visiting film stars and authors are often accompanied by 'clipboard Nazis', who make a big deal of the conditionality of the access you have been granted to the VIP, stating in advance that you may not ask specific questions. Depending on the VIP's recent history, those questions might relate to their marriage, the ailment from which their child suffers, a recent court case or that picture taken of them in a loo with a rolled-up fifty Euro note. If you agree to do an interview while avoiding an area you know your readers want to know about – and you may have to – the fact is that you are effectively doing PR for the VIP, not journalism. In this situation, a good journalist will do a wide-eyed absorption of the conditions but never verbally agree that they definitely won't ask a particular question. The clipboard Nazis rarely seek such an undertaking, because they usually sit in on the interview and throw their bodies in front of the oncoming train, putting up a traffic-cop hand to warn the VIP against answering while gesturing towards the door with the other hand, meaning, 'You: get out.' To cope with this situation, you follow Mitford's guidelines and get your interviewee talking about attitudes and behaviours parallel to but not directly related to the issue, then ask them to compare and contrast what they have just said with the proscribed area. If they retreat behind the clipboard Nazi, keep the recorder going and make notes of precisely what they do. They may decide to answer. But even their refusal to answer – whether it's furious or just bored, active or passive – can provide an angle for your story. Plan ahead so that if you get thrown out at this point, you have enough material to make a worthwhile feature anyway.

No question is unaskable. You may decide that a question is tacky or tasteless or invasive but do not project your feelings on to your interviewee. If your readers want the answer to the question, your first duty is to them. Like any journalist, I have had to ask people about their sex lives, their terminal illnesses, their personal failures, their addictions, enemies and tragedies. I have never had an interviewee refuse to answer a question, which is the great fear of most interviewers.

What has happened to me, and is much more difficult to deal with than a straightforward refusal, is where an interviewee begins to weep. One woman talked to me about the drug addiction of her teenage son and as I probed the issue, began to cry. I kept going. So did she. I mentioned how upset she was in the feature and she wrote to thank me, not just for representing her truthfully, but for listening to her, rather than telling her he would be all right.

Listening means you catch inconsistencies. If, for example, an interviewee talks freely about the 1990s, then skips to 2004, the chances are that in the beginning of the twenty-first century they were in prison or in hospital or somewhere else worth exploring.

If you plan to be a good profile writer, you simply cannot afford to dress up the desire to keep yourself safe as sensitivity toward your interviewee. Freelances who do not make it as interviewers often fail because they are too focused on themselves and their feelings and pay too little attention to the wonderful possibilities of discovery, if the person sitting opposite is interviewed with genuine curiosity and matching courtesy.

When you leave the interview, sit in your car afterwards in silence. No radio on. No mobile phone calls. No texts. Just sit there dreaming. Walk through the interview in your head. Just that. Walk through the sequence as you remember it. Descriptions, insights and inconsistencies may strike you. Write them down. Do it before you transcribe your recording.

Now you have the raw material for your profile. All you have to do is write it.

8

WRITING PROFILES

I improve on misquotation.

Cary Grant

These are the four essential building blocks of a good personality profile:

- Biographical details
- Quotations
- Descriptions
- Judgement

BIOGRAPHICAL DETAILS
Biographical details are the important points in a human beings life, not the details you find on a tombstone or a curriculum vitae.

Tombstones detail the least illustrative points of an individual's life: when they were born and when they died. CVs detail the educational achievements and employment pattern of someone, together with statements about whether or not they hold a clean driver's licence and can drum up credible support from prestigious referees. Neither tells the reader anything about the essence or the personality of the person.

Too many profiles follow the tombstone and CV models, giving the date of birth as if it had a breath-holding significance. Unless someone was born in the middle of a hurricane or at precisely the moment the first plane hit the Twin Towers, the date has little significance to anybody other than the person who arrived into the human family on that particular date. Profiles then tend to move on to chronological recounting of the subject's passage through life, missing the point that it's not what happens to a man or woman but what they do with what happens to them that matters. Whenever a profile-writer finds themselves telling the reader that their interviewee went to a particular school in 1968 and graduated a few years later, the writer should realise that they are concentrating – mistakenly – on the scaffolding, not on the building itself. The reader wants to know about successes and failures, crises and challenges, triumphs and disasters, learning and losses. Each of these must be discovered throughout the profile, and dogged fidelity to the chronology of someone's life is rarely the best way to discover their reality.

Chronology is one persuasive distraction from the deeper truth you want to deliver in a profile. Data is another. Of course, the profile writer must be accurate but accuracy does not require that you become mastered by the facts. For example, if you are told that in a particular year your subject changed career direction, what matters is not the day, month and year or indeed the raw fact itself but the person or people or circumstances that influenced them to make the shift. Human beings are always gripped by conversions, whether dramatic, as in Saul falling off his horse on the way to

Damascus and rising up a Christian, or more gradual. Points of learning and change in a profile fascinate readers.

We are hooked by before and after sagas, so the profile writer, alerted to a quantum shift in life pattern on the part of the subject, should immediately start rooting for contrasts: what was it, in their life before the change, that ripened and readied them for something new? In the process of illustrating their before and after, you will find yourself revealing their attitudes to family, homeplace, money, boredom and work.

While I hang a caveat on the advisability of sedulously recounting the subject's life in chronological sequence, this does not mean that beginning at the start and continuing to the present day is necessarily a bad approach. It isn't. Going back through the elicited details of someone's life may convince you that following it chronologically is the best way to illustrate their growth, setbacks, breakthroughs and points of great sadness. No problem. Just make sure that the biographical details do not move centre-stage. Wherever possible, present biographical data on the run.

Not:

'He took a BA degree in DCU in 2003,'

but:

'A BA degree from DCU launched him into his career with the hope of...'

Above all, be wary of repetitive phrases, which the chronological approach tends to provoke. If one sentence starts, 'In 2003, he set off for Australia,' that's fine. If the next paragraph begins, 'In 2005, he was deported from Oz,' we will live with it. If the following sentence opens with, 'In 2006, he was back in Drimnagh,' we will get bored with him and with you.

QUOTATIONS

The second pivotal element in any profile is allowing the reader to hear the voice of the individual and get a sense of the language they use. A personality feature without quotations is essentially an essay rather than a profile. The essay is a quite legitimate and currently under-utilised form of journalism, but it puts the personality on a fairly static plane. Allowing the individual to be heard, in their own language, reveals an essential facet of their personality, background and current reality, since each of us uses language in a way that's arguably as unique as are our fingerprints.

This is where the tape recorder can – in its faithful rendition of the subject's way of talking, offer a challenge to the writer, who may want to tidy up their sometimes scattered syntax. Here's an example: 'I'll never accept it. I'll never, ever accept Jamie's death, not as long as I live. Never. His books, his briefcase – everything belonging to him hanging around the house just jolts me every day.'

The essayist will not use the quotation in any form but will simply allude to the fact that the death of the woman's son is never far from her mind. The neatnik journalist may tidy it up, so it becomes this: 'I will never accept the death of my son. His possessions in my home are a constant reminder.'

That version is undoubtedly neater and clearer – and markedly less evocative. The contractions are gone. Instead of 'I'll,' we get, 'I will,' which is more formal. The repetitions are gone. But repetitions can contribute to the delivery of a cluster of meaning, in a way impossible for a single sentence which is spare and correct in structure. The one-word, verbless sentence ('Never.') is gone. Yet most people, when they're talking, use single-word verbless sentences, no matter how technically incorrect they may be, for the purposes of emphasis. The name of the boy is gone, reducing him to a category. Worst of all, the specifics are gone. Whereas the reader can see the book and imagine the briefcase, a reference to 'his possessions' is not only vague but too formal to stimulate the imagination into working on precisely what these possessions might be.

Good profiles capture the way their subjects talk. Tidying up a quotation is permissible, as long as the sense remains the same, if the tidying removes the ems and ahs which might make the subject look, in print, moronic. But that's it. Changing the sense in any way is not acceptable. (What you do with profanities depends entirely on the house style of the newspaper or magazine to which you intend to submit the piece. Some like to include every swear-word as uttered, whereas others either water them down, using 'f***' rather than the whole word, and some remove them entirely.)

Do not kid yourself that you have a quotation when all you have set down is a snippet. Here is a snippet in ineffectual action: 'She talked haltingly about her son, Jamie, who died at seventeen in a car crash. She recalls him, she says, daily, when she sees his belongings "hanging around the house".'

A snippet is too short to allow us to hear the real voice of your interviewee, and too imprecise to allow us to differentiate between your interviewee and all others. Give good substantial chunks of quotations and attribute them simply. People usually say something or comment on an issue. They don't rebut or refute or flout or retort or snort or smirk their observations. When attributing quotations, the best advice is the old American acronym of KISS, meaning Keep It Simple, Stupid.

Once you have established the voice of your interviewee and you have also made it clear that nobody else is speaking, then you can insert perhaps the fourth block of quoted material without a separate attribution. Just indent the first line of it, as you will indent the first line of each quotation, put quote marks around it, and leave it alone.

If you get really good, thought-provoking quotations, you can use one of them as an introduction to the feature, if the publication for which you are writing favours that approach. Or incorporate it into your headline. Or finish the profile with it.

DESCRIPTIONS

The third pillar supporting a good profile is the visual. The reader must see the man or woman about whom they're reading, and this applies even if the feature is accompanied by a photograph. In some cases, the photograph may be a stock shot, or may be so carefully posed as to give no insight into what this girl or fella is like when they're not acting a role for a camera. It is important, therefore, whether or not a picture accompanies your article, to give a visual sense of the encounter.

That requires abandonment of the kind of factual details adopted by the Garda Síochána when they issue a missing person's announcement. These details defy the most imaginative listener's attempt to get a picture of the lost soul: 'Just over five feet, of slim build, wearing a black jacket and dark shoes.' Personalities should be so described that the reader sees them as if at the centre of a brightly lit stage, moving, talking, gesturing, reacting.

The existing public perception is the ideal starting point

for any description of a famous personality. The writer can choose to prove the public perception wrong ('You think this guy is a nerdy little dude, but he's really a super-cool hunk.') or confirm it, or, in confirming the perception, provide added facets to it. Most TV viewers have a version of Miriam O'Callaghan that goes down only as far as the waist, at which point she's cut off by the desk she's sitting behind. They may not understand how astonishingly tall she is, or realise that, off-screen, she's casually informal enough to run along the corridors of RTÉ barefoot.

Remember that, even if your subject appears on TV several times a week, what the reader wants to know is whether this version of them matches the one you encounter. Do they move differently from the prescribed way they move on TV? Do they speak at a different pace when they're not reading off Speech Que?

Describing someone requires observation, accuracy – and kindness. Eugene Meyer, who owned *The Washington Post* more than a hundred years ago, drew up a set of principles for his paper, which have some relevance in the area of profile writing, even though we live in radically different times.

'As a disseminator of news,' Meyer wrote, 'the paper shall observe the decencies that are obligatory upon a private gentleman. What it prints shall be fit reading for the young as well as for the old.'

Or, to quote the title of one of Peter Ustinov's short stories, add a dash of pity. A dash of pity was noticeably missing from the opening of an otherwise superb profile by a writer who shall be nameless. 'Father Joe Bloggs has long, brown teeth,' it began.

Good observation. Joe Bloggs has outstandingly long,

brown teeth. But as the opening to a profile for which he had given the writer an interview? Come on.

On the other hand, when a writer profiling me for the *Sunday Tribune* described me as 'Junoesque' she did a professional job of physical delineation. Readers could work out that I was enormous. But she halted one step short of brutality.

In addition to your subject's clothes and physical demeanour, if you are interviewing them in their home or office, you should be alert for indicative clues. I don't mean that you should ask to use their bathroom in order to check out their medicine chest, or teach yourself to read the correspondence on their desk upside down, as old hacks always claimed to be able to do, but you should certainly check out the books they have, and whether they're out for display or have the scattered thumbed look of favourites.

The photographs, framed or unframed, on their desk, are relevant. The art someone has on the wall of their office or home says something about them, as do the items held on to the fridge door by magnets. Even the kind of magnets is relevant. Soak up every detail of your subject's surroundings, possessions and props during the interview. What do they touch and how do they touch it?

You might find that what looks like a watch for display is in fact part of their diving gear – and that nobody knew they went diving. Jewellery is another clue. Inexpensive jewelry says one thing about someone, whereas obviously expensive items say something else. Jewellery goes in cycles, so if someone is wearing a charm bracelet, the chances are that they're over sixty. Older jewellery usually has a story to it, if you ask. Later you can work out the significance of the accessories, props and possessions. Just don't miss them while you're there.

JUDGEMENT

Arguably the single most difficult aspect of a profile is to provide enough information to the reader for them to make a judgement on the person being profiled. Are they likeable or dislikeable? Do they find the writer/TV presenter/singer/politician amusing, interesting, stimulating, pompous, small-minded, witty, self-absorbed or superficial?

In the course of the interview, the writer makes these judgements instinctively, amending or reinforcing them by listening to the disc and reflecting on the experience. Other factors can influence your view, including gratitude to the person for giving you their time, or to a third party who facilitated the encounter. Those factors should be consciously assessed because of the possibility of producing, not a profile, but a public relations puff piece. That happens when the writer takes on board everything the subject wants and gets ready to regurgitate it, unmediated, to the public. Good profile writers never allow themselves to be used as the conduit for a celebrity's self-confection. Your posture throughout the interview must be warmly attentive but you do not have to switch off your scepticism or discrimination.

However, having made your own decisions about the person you have interviewed, you must not lay those conclusions – negative or positive – directly on the reader. Beside me, as I write, is a profile in an English newspaper of the man they describe as 'the extremely likeable Michael Palin'. That is so directive that it may put the reader off the person. Nor is it necessary. The profile itself gives the reader the evidence on which to agree that, yes, Michael Palin is an extremely likeable person.

You may find, for example, that a personality talks a great deal about the importance of family life. Let's say he goes on at length about how he treasures his wife and children as valuable individuals. If you find yourself disbelieving this, you must interrogate the evidence. You may find, for example, that he never names them, so they figure in his discourse not as separate persons but as props to his self-regard. In which case you must find a way to juxtapose the evidence so that the reader may come to the same conclusion. What you must not do is tell the reader what to think or tell them what you think. As a profile writer, you bring a bright light to bear on your subject. You do not bore a hole in them with a laser.

If the person you profiled bores you, he or she presents you with an interesting problem. As readers, we every now and then encounter a book written about boring people, and at the end of it wonder how the writer couldn't have spotted that it's difficult to make boring people interesting. (The corollary does not hold true. It's appallingly easy to make interesting people boring either by asking them the wrong questions or writing a pallid profile about them.) You must make even the boring person interesting. Someone once said that 99 per cent of people are interesting, and that even the 1 per cent person who isn't is still interesting, because of being the exception to the rule.

You, as the profile writer, are there to showcase the person you interview. If they disappoint you, or have damn all to say for themselves, write a profile that shows how flaccid they really are. Be entertaining about the contrast between their public image and their boring reality. But don't just transport boredom from one location to another. Or take refuge in pointing out that the feature is accurate and truthful. If readers wanted truth and truth alone, they could buy the periodic census report from the Central Statistics Office.

This does not mean that you can write about your feelings prior to the interview, during the interview and after the interview. We, the readers, do not care about your feelings unless you are a profile writer so famous in your own right that the reader is just as interested in the writer as in what he or she is writing about. Keep yourself offstage and find a way to shine a bright light on your subject.

Dos and Don'ts of getting a personality profile right

- *Do* let us hear the personality speaking in their own words.
- *Do* give us a sense of what they look like and to what degree they displace air in the room.
- *Do* give us the evidence on which we can make a judgement or come to a conclusion about them.
- *Do* get the facts right about them.
- *Do* make sure that your readers share your experience in its best light.
- *Don't* record what the personality says and then paraphrase it.
- *Don't* tell us what to think, Show us the evidence and leave us to make up our own minds.
- *Don't* write a PR puff piece. Present the personality to us, warts and all, light and shade.
- *Don't* give us tombstone details. Give us details of progress and setbacks, triumphs and disasters – and how the subject coped with them.

- *Don't* recycle material from the internet. No matter how long the person has been on the road or how many times they have been interviewed or profiled, they are different today from what they were yesterday and it's up to you to find how that difference shows and make us care about it and them.

9

WRITING A NOVEL

*Your Manuscript is both good and original, but
the part that is good is not original and the part
that is original is not good.*

Samuel Johnson

You start writing a novel when two things come together:
your idea of what a novel should be and your sense that
you can produce one. If you believe that a novel should be a
coruscating construct of language and glancing images, you
cannot start writing that novel until you have the skills to
deliver on the ambitious self-set task.

Each of us has our own definition of what constitutes a
novel. Here's one, from John Gardner, a critic, poet and
novelist who specialised in the teaching of creative writing
and who wrote a book called *On Becoming a Novelist*.

> Normal people, people who haven't been misled
> by a faulty college education, do not read
> novels for words alone. They open a novel with
> the expectation of finding a story, hopefully
> with interesting characters in it, possibly an

interesting landscape here and there and, with any luck at all, an idea or two – with real luck a large and interesting cargo of ideas.

Though there are exceptions, as a rule the good novelist does not worry primarily about linguistic brilliance – at least not brilliance of the showy, immediately obvious kind – but instead worries about telling his story in a moving way, making the reader laugh or cry or endure suspense, whatever it is that this particular story, told at its best, will incline the reader to do.

We read five words on the first page of a really good novel and we begin to forget that we are reading printed words on a page. We begin to see images – a dog hunting through garbage cans, a plane circling above Alaskan mountains, an old lady furtively licking her napkin at a party. We slip into a dream, forgetting the room we're sitting in, forgetting it's lunchtime or time to go to work. We recreate, with minor and for the most part unimportant changes, the vivid and continuous dream the writer worked out in his mind (revising and revising until he got it right) and captured in language so that other human beings, whenever they feel like it, may open his book and dream that dream again…

Gardner's use of the male pronoun is typical of the time in which he wrote – thirty years ago. But the sketch of the magic of a novel, whether high art or low entertainment, is timelessly relevant. John Steinbeck agreed with Gardner's emphasis on anecdote: 'I can't think of anything else necessary to a writer except a story and the will and the ability to tell it,' he wrote in his *Journal of a Novel*, the book that started out as a series of letters to his editor, Pascal Covici, throughout 1951, recording his experiences as he wrote the first draft of *East of Eden*. Steinbeck had a plan for the novel and believed such a plan was necessary before writing should begin. He wrote to his editor:

> I judge that this book will have in it roughly 110 thousand words. With slips that will take about sixty working days and of course there are bound to be days lost besides the weekends. So I rather think, barring accidents, by the first of July I shall have half the book done...

The final novel had within it several of these 'books' but the journal of how he wrote it portrays him as workmanlike in his daily delivery of a set number of pages, handwritten, using pencils with soft leads, which gave him calluses on his 'writing finger'. Steinbeck's constant concern – one he assuredly does not share with more modern writers working against a deadline – was to prevent himself going too fast and making too much progress. Only by writing slowly did he believe he could stay in control of the massy bulk of his material and the complex cast of characters.

One of the most endearing aspects of Steinbeck's letters is the dread of finishing the novel they reveal on his part. He was in love with it as he wrote it, and loath to finish with it. He complained, as do all writers, of sore hands, backache and headaches, but regarded all of them as preferable to the alternative: 'One is never drained by work but only by idleness,' he reflected. 'Lack of work is the most enervating thing in the world.'

No writer I have ever met, including those producing what would be regarded as facile formulaic bestsellers, finds the task easy. Barbara Taylor Bradford, who wrote a string of international bestsellers, likens her work to slaving in a salt mine:

> I sit long hours at my desk, starting out at six in the morning and finishing around six or seven in the evening. And I do this six and a half days a week, till my neck and shoulders seize up. I make tremendous social and personal sacrifices for my writing, but after all, I chose to be a novelist. Nobody held a gun to my head.

Nobody holds a gun to any writer's head but maybe they should hold one to their own head, at least until they have a solid work plan in place.

First of all, determine how long the book will be. The average mystery novel runs about 200 pages in manuscript, but a straight novel can be something as slim as 200 pages or as fat as 700. You are the only person who can figure how many pages you will need to tell this story. Take out your calculator. Are you writing a three-hundred-page novel? OK. How many chapters will you need? The length of each chapter will be determined by how much you have to say in that chapter. If you're depicting the Battle of Waterloo, it might be a trifle difficult to compress it into ten pages. If you're writing about a man putting out the garbage, you probably have only a scene and you'll need additional scenes to make a full chapter.

How you approach your first novel depends on you and your surrounding circumstances. My first – *The Scattering of Mrs Blake* – published by Marion Boyars in London, started because Louis Lentin, then Head of Drama in RTÉ television, commissioned a television play for me and, when I submitted the first draft, asked me a million questions about the motivation driving individual characters to take particular actions. Because I so often found myself looking at him blankly, I decided the best thing to do would be to write a novel which would provide all the explanations. The novel was published. The TV play was never broadcast, although I did get paid for it, because Louis resigned from RTÉ and moved on to other projects, including the docudrama about Goldenbridge Orphanage.

Most novels get written because writers cannot *not* write them. They get written without any sense of sales or markets. They pour out in a form of self-expression, and only after they are complete does the novelist consider a possible publisher. The majority of novels written go unpublished. Only a lucky minority make it into print. Some of the best do not. Publishers get it wrong – as the countless stories of success, critical validation and bestseller status according to frequently rejected novels establishes. Sometimes, when they get it wrong, they crush a potentially great writer into silence, and nobody will ever know how often that has happened.

Resilient writers keep going. Stephen King, one of the most prolific and bestselling modern authors, had his first four novels rejected by publishers. When he finished the fifth, he didn't even bother submitting it, turfing it directly into the waste-paper basket. His wife Tabitha pulled it out, read it and told him he was wrong and should submit it. In 1973, Doubleday accepted it and brought it out as *Carrie*.

If publishers get it wrong, writers get it wrong, too. A writer who falls in love with a particular kind of bestseller and decides to produce their personal version of the genre may find that by the time they have the manuscript finished, the vogue for this particular kind of writing has evaporated.

The novels which quite decidedly signal 'Don't publish me' come in many forms. I have just finished reading two such manuscripts. One is a sequel to a bestselling novel of the sixties. Now, quite apart from the rights issues implicit in taking someone else's characters and moving them on in age, this novel will never be published because nobody remembers the earlier bestseller and the sequel, to work at all, requires the reader to have been enthralled by that book.

The second manuscript will not be published because it is essentially a plan for a novel, rather than a novel itself. It describes what happens to named people, but is written like an extended report. No scenes happen that we can see. No conversations happen that we can hear. Nothing takes life in front of our eyes, nothing engages our emotions, so only a reader with an oversized sense of duty would plough right through it to the conclusion.

Another kind of novel which rarely makes it onto the bookshelves is the thinly disguised autobiography of someone who has not lived a life which is interesting to other people. Every individual's life is interesting to themselves. We are all centre-stage in the drama of our own existence. But when a writer cannot create the same excitement in a reader that they feel about their own experiences, the book sits dead in the water, never to float.

Christopher Derrick, a publisher's reader who ploughed his way through many a submitted manuscript, has a pet list of unpublishable novel types, including what he calls the Painfully Irish Novel, the elements of which he sums up thus:

> Glory and heartbreak of wild uproarious youth in Dublin, with students and poets and poverty and fine whirling talk and Guinness and the Gardaí and people being sick at parties, and mad-eyed mistresses and dotty peers, and great crumbling Georgian mansions…

Of course, no writer every believes that what they have produced is boring, clichéd or unpublishable, so, if you are convinced you are tomorrow's Joseph O'Connor, Sebastian Barry, Anne Enright or Cecelia Ahern, what you want to know is how to get your wonderful work to the people who will put it in print or help to put it in print.

The traditional approach to submitting a novel is to send a book proposal to an agent or publisher. Many publishers now provide on their websites a questionnaire designed to guide prospective novelists in the preparation of such a proposal which typically comprises:

- An outline on a single page, taking no more than 300 words
- A statement about the market, indicating what kind of reader would buy this book and why it would attract them
- An indication as to why the writer should be taken seriously: giving details of, say, their

publication of short stories or other material
- A plan for the book, giving an insight into the central characters, how the plot will develop, key lines of tension within it while also stating how long it will be and when it will be completed
- An undertaking to promote the book if required
- An outline of the chapters
- One sample chapter

Up to relatively recently, this was the only way to suss out if a publisher would take a look at a longer manuscript. However, many publishers now, particularly in Ireland, have moved beyond that approach, which made more sense in the days of big advances which allowed the novelist to abandon the day job and devote themselves to competing the text. Today, big advances for first novels are rare. In Ireland, they almost never happen.

Where a novel is concerned, particularly if it is a popular or 'chick-lit' offering, a publisher is much more likely to want the complete manuscript. This way they can get a real sense of its possibilities, and have the comfort of knowing they do not have the worry of announcing a newcomer's work to the trade, only to find that the newcomer cannot deliver during the limited period of time within which the trade stays enthusiastic.

We will come to the function of agents later on in this book, but, assuming you choose the direct route to a publisher and get amazingly lucky, the word may come back from them indicating that they would like to bring out your book.

Your day is made. Your week is made. Your whole life feels improved. Control yourself and concentrate on the conditionality of the communication. What you hear is that the publisher intends to bring out your book. What the publisher may actually say is that, subject to your agreeing to some rewriting, they will issue a contract and bring out your book.

Rewriting happens when the publisher puts an editor to work on your text and the euphoria of acceptance and impending publication carries the writer through the first raft of queries and objections. It may even carry them through the second draft. But by the time the third set arrives, the writer may be in a funk and have developed a pathological hatred of the editor.

The function of a publisher's editor is to make sure the story of your novel tells itself in the best possible way. So they will draw your attention to a character who is insufficiently developed and rather one-dimensional. They may object to longueurs in the manuscript which do not, in their view, contribute to the whole. They may redline a series of clichés and pet phrases you a) never knew were clichés or b) never knew you repeated so frequently. Novelist Peter De Vries once said that, while he loved being a writer, what he couldn't stand was the paperwork, and most writers heartily agree with him. Few are lucky enough to have an editor like Max Perkins, who nursed Hemingway, Scott Fitzgerald and several other writers along so that each produced the best work of which they were capable. Perkins was a combination of cheerleader, money-lender, marriage counsellor and literary gold-miner. Today's editors are more hurried, more focused on commercial concerns (like getting the book on to the bestseller list) and may be less personally committed to each of the stable of writers with whom they work.

Most novels are extensively reworked between submission and publication. Potential conflict with the editor can be mitigated in advance if, prior to submitting the book, you first reread it as critically as you can, watching for and excising any self-indulgence like phrases present for no purpose other than that you like them, or characters irrelevant to the thrust of the work. Watch out for facetiousness and for anything contrivedly funny or sad. Read the manuscript as if you were someone else, and assess how the tone of the writer strikes you. Are you, as the reader, being talked down to? Or bossed? Or wooed too obviously?

Before you go to work with an editor, a large vaccination of humility helps. As does the constant reminder to yourself that the editor would not be working on your book unless they liked it and wanted it to be as good as it can be. Editors have the blessing of a detachment no writer has about their own work. Their suggestions, 90 per cent of the time, improve the end result. If they propose something that would, in your view, tear the lights and liver out of your novel, don't accept that suggestion. But never underestimate the value of a good editor.

After the editor and you have come to agreement on the manuscript, or even while you are in the process of agreeing, it will go to the designer, whose task is to come up with a cover.

This happens very quickly, because the promotion/sales departments of publishers like to have proofs and jackets as early as possible so that they can alert booksellers to the impending publication of the book. They are likely to show you the jacket design, but not to give you power of veto over it. So even international bestseller Germaine Greer found one of her books selling in a jacket she truly hated because, she felt, it contradicted the essence of the book. Most writers fight with the design of the cover of their book. Few of them win, because publishers believe they know the market better than writers do. This is questionable. Publishers do all sorts of daft things in the interests of selling big numbers of a title.

Rewrites should happen after a contract is issued, because you do not want to completely recast your work and then find the publisher has gone off it anyway.

The contract, when it arrives, is in impenetrably legal language and nearly as long as the book itself. A first novelist, thrilled by the prospect of being published, is likely to sign the contract and send it back the following day. This is particularly so if the contract is not just for the manuscript they submitted, but is a 'three-book deal', which promises publication of two further novels after that first. Much of the grief, bitterness and legal hassle in which writers and publishers too frequently become enmeshed would be prevented if writers were not so recklessly grateful when they get that initial contract.

Before you sign any contract, show it to a lawyer with experience of intellectual property rights and publishing. Show it to an agent – remembering that an agent gets much more interested in you when you arrive on their doorstep with a contract in hand, because then they do not have to sell you; all they have to do is take care of you. Show it to a friend who has been published already. But do not simply sign it and trust that all will be well.

Generally speaking, a publisher should offer you a royalty of ten per cent of the selling price of a hardback book on the first 5000 sold, more for subsequent copies. (One in a hundred first novels reaches these figures. And in Ireland, at the moment, roughly the same number of first novels get into hardback in the first place.)

Paperback royalties are lower, typically starting at 7.5 per cent.

If the royalty seems small, remember that 35-55 per cent of the retail price of every book goes to the bookseller, 10-15 per cent per cent to the printer and binder, and about 10 per cent on sales and distribution, including advertising costs, if any. (Few Irish publishers can afford to engage in advertising, although booksellers like Easons do.) The publisher supports editors, accountants, graphic artists and books that do not sell as well as had been hoped. In addition, they have to send out free copies for review. So 10 per cent is not bad, and if you are offered less, as you will be if they plan to bring your novel out in paperback, it is worth considering the fact that the publisher is investing money in your product, at what may turn out to be considerable risk.

However, do not let your gratitude blind you to what rights you may be signing away. Contracts for books which could, conceivably, be filmed, serialised, published in paperback, translated, broadcast or televised should contain provision for all such 'subsidiary rights'. Some authors like to retain such rights but a publisher may see their only hope of profit in them. One book I published had excerpts sold to several overseas newspapers and magazines, including *Reader's Digest,* and, as a result, I made a little profit, as did the publisher, even though the book itself did not hit the bestseller lists. I was fortunate that the publisher had put clauses in the contract giving me a generous proportion of this kind of earnings. Fortunate, because the earlier advice on reading your contract comes under the heading of, 'Do as

I say, not as I do.' I've never in my life read a book contract or asked a lawyer to look at one for me and appreciate that I've been unbelievably lucky not to have trackmarks left on my wallet by any of the five publishers I've worked with.

The publisher should offer at least 60 per cent of revenue from subsidiary rights (such as those mentioned) to the author.

A clause governing revision of rights is also important. That means an agreement giving rights back to the author if the publisher lets the book go out of print for longer than a specified time.

Remember that the law assumes the copyright in anything you have written is yours, and that you assign to the publisher only certain defined rights to publish in particular forms, particular parts of the world and within particular periods. An agreement that assigns the whole copyright in return for a lump sum or an ill-defined royalty is rarely in the author's best interest.

All this applies to smaller pieces of work, too. It is no harm, for instance, to acknowledge a payment for a short story with the observation that it is in respect of 'first serial rights'. If you do not do this, you could give some little magazine an income for life from Hollywood. *Brokeback Mountain*, for example, was based, not on a novel but on a short story, although Annie Proulx has been around long enough to have taken care of her rights in the event of a movie being mooted.

When you are pursuing this, if you do not have a manager (as does Roddy Doyle), an agent or a lawyer on the job, be businesslike but not neurotic. Publishers quickly tire of writers who become obsessive about retaining Japanese or Croatian rights.

In among all the horrible rejections and even more ghastly things many writers experience when their manuscripts are accepted comes the odd shining exception, like Ciara Geraghty, who admits she's had 'quite a nice time' getting published.

The first advantage Ciara has is a sister named Niamh, whom she describes as instrumental in the entire project, always encouraging, always certain that Ciara's book would be published and would sell.

Ciara produced three chapters and a friend then sent the sample to an Irish publisher, who expressed interest but wanted to see ten more. When the ten went to the publisher, they said the book needed fleshing out and a lot more work. Collapse of confidence. But then Ciara got her act together, finished the book and decided to get an agent. Four agents based in Ireland were listed in the *Writers' and Artists' Yearbook*, so, one afternoon, she rang all four. One said to post the manuscript to him. Three were out of their offices. She left messages. One, Ger Nichol, who runs the Book Bureau, rang back in half an hour, read the book overnight, and agreed to represent Ciara the next day. Ger sent the manuscript to Hodder (now Hachette Ireland) and they came back with 'a fantastic two-book deal'.

Up to that point, writing had been Ciara's secret. She had three small children and worked in insurance, writing at night when the kids were asleep and early in the morning, always hoping for eventual publication. This happened in August 2008. She admits that things changed at this point:

> Now, I was contracted to write another book, and
> that was quite difficult. I wrote my first novel,

Saving Grace, in the comfort of my own home on
my own time, in the dead of night. In my daily life,
I was Average Jo, mother of three, insurance clerk.
I loved that about it. The secret was out when the
book was published. The nature of conversations I
had with people changed. I was on maternity leave
when I wrote it, too, and that was tricky enough –
as was the pressure to deliver on a deadline.

When the second book was complete, she attended the
London Book Fair, where it created much interest. A week
later, her publishers offered a second two-book contract: 'That
allowed me to give up my proper job and dedicate myself to
writing.'

By the time she was two-thirds of the way through the third
novel, she realised that she was finding dedicated writing a
much more enjoyable experience. She works from nine in the
morning until lunchtime. Niamh, her sister, minds her baby
and the older children are at school during that time.

While Ciara has had a remarkably positive experience, she
has also had to face the hammering a second novel gets. (First
novels often get a free pass from reviewers.):

I did take negative reviews very personally. I very
much took them to heart. It's like someone saying
your baby is very ugly. But it didn't take long for
the skin to toughen up. You just have to man up
and take it on the chin. The main advice I'd give
to new writers is, 'Don't show your work to people
too early.' Have a great body of work done and
be absolutely delighted with it before you hand

it to people. I know people who have not got good feedback early on in writing, and have been totally dispirited. Writing a book is like running a marathon. You have to have stamina.

The title is one of the issues to be negotiated with your publisher before your novel (or non-fiction book) is published. A great title can communicate the essence of a book instantaneously, or create curiosity. It is much easier to produce a good title for a non-fiction book like *Fast Food Nation* or *The Boss* than it is to come up with a good title for a work of fiction. One of the worst titles I ever came across is the single-word *Gilead*. If I hadn't already fallen in love with its writer, Marilynne Robinson, I would never have considered buying the novel.

Titles have always been problematic for writers, although. Herbert Bayard Swope, one of the first reporters in New York to get a byline, back in the 1920s, was a great self-marketer who is credited by historian Mike Dash (in *Satan's Circus*) with being, 'the first writer to use the word "Inside" in the title of a book to denote exclusive or privileged access – a device that has been widely copied since.'

John Steinbeck went through a number of possible titles for one of his novels, including *The Salinas Valley* and *Cain Sign*. Transcribing the sixteen verses in *Genesis* about Cain and Abel to help him over a hump in the writing, he encountered the last three words of the final verse.

'I think I have a title at last,' he wrote to his editor the following day. 'A beautiful title, *East of Eden...*'

10

Writing a Non-Fiction Book

Every time a friend succeeds, I die a little.

Gore Vidal

It is easier now than at any stage in the past to submit a non-fiction book to an international or an Irish publisher, if only because any publisher worth the name has a comprehensive website which gives a clear picture of what they publish and what they do not publish. Thereby reducing the amount of ill-directed tosh landing on their desk. Thereby giving them the time to pay attention to a professionally-presented manuscript, even if it lands on their desk rather than being carried in for presentation in the white-gloved hands of a literary agent.

Any writer who has a book in them should check out these websites. For one thing, they leave the site-visitor in no doubt as to what they publish and what they do not publish. New writers tend to think of publishers as a single type: they bring out books. Of course they do, but each brings out a different kind of book. Some are general publishers. Some publish fiction only. Some publish only school or legal or accountancy textbooks. Some, like Londubh Books, the publisher of the book you're reading, do no fiction, concentrating on non-fiction and only on subjects of interest to an Irish readership. Send a fiction, poetry or children's book proposal to Londubh Books and you've wasted your time and theirs.

Most Irish publishers, whether of fiction or non-fiction, will look at a proposal or manuscript sent by post or email. They may not exactly encourage unsolicited manuscripts, but generally speaking, they don't ignore them. Their websites will often elucidate their preferences. The Londubh site, for example, reminds writers to include their contact details with anything sent.

'If someone has a complete manuscript, I'd like to see that, in addition to their one-page summary and CV,' says Jo O'Donoghue of Londubh Books. 'If you'd like us to return your manuscript please include adequate return postage with your submission. Unfortunately it is not usually possible for us to provide feedback when we reject a manuscript.'

The first step you can take in rejection-prevention is to present your manuscript the way your chosen publisher prefers. Below is what Jo O'Donoghue has laid down as her 'house style':

1. PRESENTATION OF MANUSCRIPTS

Please submit your manuscript on a CD or as an email attachment to jo@londubh.ie. You may need to submit a printout or even a marked-up printout if the layout of your book is complicated, for instance if it contains graphs or tables or if there are several levels of headings.

Please do not: use double spaces after full stops; use the return key at the ends of lines, except when you intend to start a new paragraph; use capitals or bold for titles, sub-titles or words to be emphasised; leave an extra line space between paragraphs (use one carriage return only).

2. CAPITAL LETTERS

Modern usage is not to capitalise words such as nationalist, summer, east, government, civil service.

In general, use capital letters:

a)   for proper names.

b)   for full titles, e.g. Cardinal Sean Brady of Armagh, President Obama, but use lower case when these words are used in a general sense, e.g. In Ireland a new president is elected every seven years.

c)   for terms such as Catholic, Protestant, Christian, Jewish, Presbyterian, Anglican, Baptist, whether as nouns or as adjectives referring to religious denominations.

d)   for specific geographic locations, e.g. the Wicklow Mountains, the River Shannon, County Kerry

e) for specific historical events of significance, e.g. the Reformation, the Second World War (do not use the form World War I/II), the 1916 Rising, the French Revolution

3. QUOTATIONS

We use single quotation marks (double within single).

Keep short quotations within the text and enclose in single quotation marks. Enclose quotations within quotations in double quotation marks.

Separate longer quotations from the main text by an extra line above and below. (They will also be indented when typeset.) In this case, do not use quotation marks. Use single quotation marks for quotes within quotes in this style.

4. NUMERALS

Spell out numerals up to one hundred in full, except where they are dates.

Fractions should also be spelled out: two-thirds, one-eighth

Our preferred form for percentages is this: 35 per cent (except in tables)

5. DATES

Use: 27 August 2002. Remember also it should be 1960s, not 1960's.

Do not use superscript for 'th' in centuries although your word processor may want to: 19th century is the preferred form.

6. ABBREVIATIONS

Do not punctuate acronyms such as SIPTU, RTÉ, USA, NAMA.

Punctuate but do not space initials: W.B.Yeats, T.K. Whitaker

Do not punctuate contractions such as St (Saint) or Dr. We spell out words like (Liffey) Street or County (Cork).

7. SPELLING

Use -ise instead of -ize in words such as realise.

Use enquiry rather than inquiry, judgement rather that judgment and acknowledgement rather than acknowledgment. This will often mean overriding your word processors spell check (which you should always apply before submitting a manuscript).

8. PUNCTUATION

The modern trend is for the minimum number of commas needed for clarity and readability.

When you are using inverted commas, the full point should come outside the closing inverted comma except where a full sentence is contained between the inverted commas. For example: They spoke of youth and its 'long, long thoughts'. But: 'There's no fool like an old fool.' (Note that American usage differs in this area.)

It has become standard not to punctuate addresses with full stops or commas.

It is perfectly acceptable to use both colons and semi-colons if you know how to use them.

9. POSSESSIVE APOSTROPHES

Use an 's' even when the name ends in 's', e.g. Yeats's house. The exceptions are Moses and Jesus.

10. HYPHENATION

Hyphenate compound words as required for clarity and readability. A good spelling dictionary such as the Oxford Spelling Dictionary will provide guidance on this and on matters to do with variant spelling and capitalisation.

11. CORRECTIONS OF PROOFS

Standard proofing marks are readily available for download on the internet if you wish to use them. You may, however, mark your proofs (in hard copy) in any legible way. The governing principle is that every change you wish to make should be clearly understandable to the person applying the corrections.

FINALLY

The most important thing is to be consistent in the use of capital letters, the presentation of quotations and in spelling and in punctuation.

Please be sure to ask us if you have any technical queries or problems with style. Get in touch with Londubh Books publisher Jo O'Donoghue: jo@londubh.ie

When you look at this house style on the company's website, it looks warm, welcoming, simple and problem-solving. When you apply it to your manuscript, it is exigent, tedious and repetitive. Tough. Someone has to do it and the publisher (any publisher, not just Jo O'Donoghue) would prefer if the writer did it. I mean, they really would prefer if you did it. This preference is so strong that receiving a manuscript which breaks all the rules may demotivate them. Why? Because the information is accessible to the writer. So if they have not bothered to incorporate it in their work, they are either so wide-blue-yonder that they're going to be difficult to deal with or so disorganised that, even if their MS is accepted, someone within the publishing house will have to spend days doing it for them.

Inevitably, publishers make exceptions for sure-fire best-selling authors like Maeve Binchy, who cheerfully admits that she writes the way she talks: 'I talk without much pause for breath and I write without much punctuation,' she confesses. 'The use of the semi-colon and the full stop and the comma wouldn't be something that I would be too familiar with…'

But she's Maeve Binchy. When you've sold as many books as she has, you'll meet with the same tolerance from your publisher. Until then, present them with pristine material.

Londubh Books puts its house style guidelines on its website, as do many other publishers, who control their temper when this free assistance is ignored by writers, as it all too frequently is. Every writer has a page format and layout with which they're comfortable. You may like your pages justified down the right hand side and your lines double-spaced. I may like unjustified pages and single-spacing. We get to indulge our individual preferences when we're drafting our work, but unless we are discourteous and have a death-wish, we take the trouble to reformat the material before we submit it, so that it meets the publisher's stated preference.

The non-academic writer who produces a successful non-fiction book is likely to be an enthusiast who can infect others with their enthusiasm. They are rarely show-offs who stud their writing with obscure terminology. (This is why I exclude academics from this area, because they come under such self-induced pressure to avoid populism.) Popular non-fiction requires the writer to use words familiar to readers who do not read very often, because they tend to be picked up by people who may not consider themselves to be readers but who become engaged in the topic. Or they may be purchased by a third party and given as a gift.

William F. Buckley, Jr, always fought this piece of advice about not using show-off words, on the basis that readers should be forced to do some work. He called less-utilised terms 'zoo words'. He wrote:

> While one can be very firm in resisting people who spout zoo words, one should be respectful and patient with those who exercise lovingly the wonderful opportunities of the language. I went

downtown some years ago to hear a black pianist about whom the word had trickled in that here was something really cool and ear-catching, besides which his name rolled about the tongue releasing intrigue and wry amusement, and so I heard Thelonious Monk. He struck some really sure-enough bizarre chords, but you know, it would never have occurred to me to walk over and say, 'Thelonious, I am not familiar with that chord you just played. So cut it out please.'

Buckley has a point. But it's a point best ignored by the writer who wants to reach an audience not currently hooked on reading. If the choice is between being impressive and selling a lot of books, keep your writing simple and you are more likely to achieve the latter. And if you want further guidance on clarity and simplicity, visit the website of the National Adult Literacy Association, NALA.

Possible topics for non-fiction books include:

- Cookery
- Crafts
- School subjects
- How-to manuals
- History
- Life and business skills
- Social Issues
- Health, diet and appearance
- Career planning
- Lists
- Children's books

(We are lumping children's books in here, even though many of them are fiction, because otherwise they will get lost.)

Cookery Books
Let us be briefly sexist. The urge to write cookery books afflicts women more than men, and it afflicts an enormous number of women. Be in no doubt. It is an affliction. Even women who don't cook that often have a hidden (and not so deeply hidden, either) thirst to see themselves and their pet recipes in print.

The first obstacle to the slaking of that thirst is that cookery books are expensive to produce, requiring great photography, full colour printing, and hardback production (because relatively few of those who will purchase a cookbook want a paperback that will fall apart under the stresses of a normal kitchen).

Publishing any 'coffee table book' which has high production values may make sense to an international publisher with a huge market and an author who is famous and photogenic, like Nigella Lawson. But even with so famous and attractive a writer, Nigella's publishers are reputed to have thought long and hard before they decided to enter the American market with her. If they won, they would have a huge win. But crossing the Atlantic, whether for fiction or non-fiction writers, is a gamble. Some novelists sell only in America. Some sell only in Europe. Some have their main market on one side of the Atlantic and do reasonably but not outstandingly well on the other side. Cookery books need to have a big market, the potential for continuing sales and the possibility of being the first of a branded series before publishers feel comfortable about investing in them.

The investment cost can be mitigated by one of several factors. The first is if the writer already has a TV series. Rachel Allen's books may not be huge bestsellers outside Ireland, but they have so solid a market within this country that producing them is worthwhile. The second way for publishers to reduce their risk is to get sponsorship. A writer who can arrive with a substantial financial guarantee from a wine seller or a cutlery-maker or a producer of cookware is going to be listened to with greater enthusiasm on the part of a potential publisher when they make their pitch to write a cookery book.

Finally, if you run a restaurant, publishing a cookbook and contributing to the cost of its production might fit with your marketing plans, and your financial contribution would make the publisher considerably more amenable to your proposal.

Crafts

The Irish market for home-grown books about embroidery, wicker-work, pottery-making, French-polishing, lace-making, crochet or knitting is remarkably small, partly because we quite suddenly stopped being full-time or part-time dressmakers or knitters about forty years ago.

America never stopped. My American agent, Tracy Brennan, undertakes all sorts of craftwork, and she would not be untypical. In any of the big American bookshops, it's possible to buy instruction books on the most abstruse crafts, just as it's possible to buy the materials for those crafts in stores like Wal-Mart.

In short, the odds against publishing an Irish craftbook are high. The odds of making money at it even higher. But exceptions happen.

School Subjects

Some of the richest writers in Ireland are not the writers you know. They are invisible, unknown teachers who produce school textbooks. If you are a teacher in a specialist area with an ability to communicate the facts about that area to young people, you might find that your knowledge could be translated into a book. Educational publishers are constantly on the hunt for new writers competent to deal with disciplines in a way that matches the constantly-changing curriculum. It is not an easy area of writing to break into, but it is easy to stay embedded once you are in.

How-to Manuals

The book you hold in your hands is a how-to manual. It sets out to meet the need of someone who wants to be a writer. How-to manuals are to be found, not just in bookshops but on the internet and in specialist shops from bait-sellers to Woodies.

The same constraints apply to many how-to manuals as to cookbooks. Trying to explain how to insert a rawl-plug is made a lot easier if the book is illustrated using graphic illustrations. These cost money to create and to print.

The key to success with a how-to manual is to ride the crest of a wave: to publish your book just as people get hooked on your theme. A couple of years ago, that theme was creative gardening, where the emphasis was not on the hassle of growing plants but on laying out the back garden in a way that, in effect, added an outdoor room to the house, decorated with the odd pot-plant (and you should hear my passionate gardener neighbour, Mary Linders, on that fashion.). Today, the emphasis is more on the interior of houses, particularly on remodelling homes, because so many couples are now stuck in a residence that no longer meets their needs but which they cannot afford to leave.

History

Serious history books tend to be commissioned by only a small number of publishers. However, if you have an insight into some oddball historical theme, it's possible to interest any non-fiction publisher. That is why books like *Cod* and *Salt* by Mark Kurlansky have been solid international sellers: they take the reader through several centuries of history through the lens of a particular product or business.

Angled history books can be written by anybody who is prepared to do the research and make the topic attractive to general readers. Biography and autobiography come under the same rules. Increasingly, in recent times, publishers have hired academics like UCD's Richard Aldous to do the research and contribute to the writing of autobiographies. In Aldous's case, the autobiography is the account of Bertie Ahern's life and political career, published in 2009.

Life and Business Skills

One way to assess the market for the book you may want to write on some life or business skill is to check what night courses are most popular in your area at this time. If people are queuing up to attend training courses in reiki or time management, it figures they will be likely to shell out for a paperback on the same topic.

That said, it should be added that every second business executive who has taken early retirement or been shed by their organisation as a result of the economic downturn seems to think they have the way, the truth and the light on a topic like leadership. Leadership, like change management, is one of those topics which attracts amateurs and bullshit in equal measure. Over the past ten years, billions have been paid by individuals and companies for courses purporting to teach both and failing to inculcate either. Let's face it, unless all the successful graduates of leadership and change management courses during that time emigrated, the courses have to have been bilge, given the shocking absence of both skills in the years since the property bubble burst...

In much the same way and in much the same period of time, a big swatch of not outstanding executives went on courses, mostly in England, to become life coaches.

The claims for life coaching are extravagant, the measurable end results less so. But now, because the life coach market is drying up, many life coaches have decided to move on to writing books about it. It is an over-supplied market. I'm sorry. This is demotivating. But the fact is that most publishers will not give serious consideration to yet another book on making lists, having goals and visualising where you want to be in five years' time, in a climate when just being alive and solvent in five years' time may be something of a challenge.

Social Issues
Social issues giving rise to books include all the 'isms:' feminism, sexism, ageism, racism. They can touch on all the phobias, from terror of wasps to fear of flying. They can encompass topics like the Church and child abuse.

A social-issues book that passes the Joe Duffy back-of-the-bus test, because it is about a topic people spontaneously discuss when they're sitting in a bus, must be published quickly. Today's social issue can become yesterday's boring topic with startling speed. Remember, it's not so long ago that the need for young couples to get on to the property ladder and the consequent demand for the abolition of property tax was a continuing controversy. Yet, just a couple of years later, a book proposal based on anything to do with property purchase is likely to give a publisher an acute case of mange.

Any topic on which you have done original research has the capacity to be explored in print. If the research is relatively minor, think about features for a newspaper. If they sell, consider expanding the topic into a book proposal. A wide range of social issues on which books could be written go unexplored, ranging from stalking to the trauma of IVF, from the social significance of fashion to the efficacy of counselling. If you have expertise on such a topic, work out what would be different and compelling about a book you might write and propose it to a non-fiction publisher.

Remember that publishers are like sharks. Just as sharks have to keep swimming in order to stay alive, so publishers have to keep publishing. Many non-fiction books earn their writers little in the way of royalties but provide them with the external credibility of being 'Author of…', which is good for the ego and can lead to other forms of employment or, if you're already in business, serve as a marketing device.

Health, Diet and Appearance
These topics are constant sellers. However, many of the same constraints apply as apply to cookbooks: you have to have external credibility, new research or a sponsor if the book is to be more than a cheap-and-cheerful paperback.

Career Planning

Since the best book on this topic has recently been published by my colleague, the Career Doctor, Eoghan McDermott (See Bibliography) I should not even mention the genre. But the fact is that this is a staple of publishing, because individuals who are starting a career, have been let go from a job or are unhappy in the post they currently hold are always eager to learn how they can improve their lot.

Lists

Every Christmas, someone comes out with a book designed to catch the eye of the impulse buyer looking for a 'stocking stuffer' present for a relative or pal who does not actually read much. Frequently, this kind of book is like *Schotts Almanac*, a random collection of often-useful data about everything and nothing.

These kinds of book can also take the form of best advice, quotations, natural ways of cleaning stained items and tips for the rearing of a happy cat/goldfish/two-year-old/golden retriever/partner/mother. Or they can be about the hundred books you must read before you die, the fifty places you must visit before ditto or the twenty best ways to save money, lose weight, declutter your home or make a nutritious meal in six minutes.

Sarah Ban Breathnach made a fortune out of *Simple Abundance* one of these impulse buy books, which require a smart idea and good production (often in an untypical or extra-small shape).

One last thought. If you have a great idea for a Christmas book, you had better have that idea at least eleven months in advance of Yule. And even at that, you may be pushing it…

Children's Books

Children's publishing is a difficult but improving area. It has always been difficult in the Irish context because to be attractive, a child's book usually requires colour presentation. The younger the reader, the greater the requirement for full-colour illustrations to help the text along. This kind of book is expensive to produce and can cost the publisher a limb if it bombs. Books aimed at those in the immediate pre-teen years and at teenagers are easier to produce because, at that stage it can be assumed that the young reader does not need illustrations quite so badly.

The most successful Irish writer of children's books in recent times, Wexford teacher Eoin Colfer, sold his *Artemis Fowl* series to an overseas publisher, Puffin, so if you think you are the next Colfer or J.K. Rowling and have within you a book which will sell all over the world, send an outline and sample chapter (or the entire manuscript) to a relevant publisher (look up *The Writer's and Artist's Yearbook* or search the internet for the right publisher or agent). In 2009 Penguin Ireland established a children's list, as did New Island (Little Island).

Publishers on the home front who bring out the occasional children's book see that a common fault in manuscripts crossing their desk is that they are written from an adult viewpoint, often by people who don't have a lot of contact with children, so are not written the way kids think or talk, right now. Oscar Wilde, whose children's books are as beautiful and relevant today as ever they were, didn't suffer from this problem. He adored his two boys, played with them constantly and told them stories. Wilde maintained that it was a mistake to 'think that children are sentimental about literature; they are not: they have humour instead.' (Roald Dahl understood this, too.)

Thomas Wright, who wrote a book about Oscar Wilde's own collection of books, noticed that the writer loved the fairy tale of the Brothers Grimm and Hans Christian Andersen. He pointed out:

> Children derive great satisfaction from the clearly defined narrative sequences of these tales with their archetypal beginnings and emphatic conclusions. The tales offer them templates for ordering their own experience – they learn to construct narratives out of everyday occurrences; to think in stories. This was a mental habit that Wilde undoubtedly acquired as a boy. Years later he told one friend that he instinctively thought in the form of stories, rather than with abstract ideas.

11

Publicising and Selling Your Book

*There are no original questions. The only way you
can do an interview is to have a conversation.
Otherwise, there's no point in doing it.*

John Banville

You've got all of the legalities right, agreed to the blurb and
had your publicity shot taken. The next step is publication
day. What the publisher decides to do, by way of promotion,
may start with a launch party, which makes the writer feel
wonderful and has little, if any, contribution to make to the
eventual sales of the book. A launch party allows the publisher
to sell copies of your book to all your friends (which I find
mortifyingly exploitative and haven't done since 1995). It
permits them to get a celebrity, usually a friend of yours, to
make a speech. Mary Finan and Albert Reynolds, when he
was Taoiseach, were good enough to appear at launches of
books I've written. The publisher may also want you to make
a speech yourself, a task that Maeve Binchy does not enjoy:

> I find it quite hard to stand up at a launch and speak
> about my book because you have to try and sell it

a bit. You can't say, 'You might like this book and you mightn't – well, give it a go anyway.' You can't say that. The publishers are sitting there steely-eyed waiting for you to say how good it is and what good value and how it is much better than the last one.

Kate Thompson, whose first novel, *It Means Mischief*, made it on to the bestseller lists, should, in theory, be well placed to shine at a launch party, since her background is in acting. (She played Terry Killeen in *Glenroe* and was best actress in the 1989 Dublin Theatre Festival.)

'I don't mind publicity tours,' she says, 'but I hate having to speak at book launches. It's a lot more difficult for an actor to stand up as themselves instead of playing a character.'

I've never understood the launch party as a publicity device, since, even if the wind is in the right direction, the best end result is when a photograph appears in the following day's newspaper. On its own, that picture will not move books. As part of a panoply of marketing activity and critical reaction, it may create what advertisers call TOMA, meaning Top Of the Mind Awareness, which can motivate buyers to go into Dubray or Waterstone's or Easons in search of the title. This marketing activity may include book signings, and appearances on media.

Writers always believe their book deserves more marketing input than it gets. The problem is that books are arguably the oddest commodity available for purchase by the general public. Some books that are never publicised achieve cult readership and eventually reach the mass market purely on word of mouth, whereas others hit the headlines on a foamy upsurge of hype and never sell at all. Some, like Joe

O'Connor's breathtaking *Star of the Sea,* sell reasonably well and are then selected for their book club by a TV programme like *Richard and Judy* (that was), resulting in a quantum leap in sales.

Book signings are sometimes used by publishers as part of a marketing campaign. I think they're weird. Just plain weird. The bookshop sets up a little table, usually where it will attract the attention of casual visitors. They may run a little banner around the table, advertising the book and its author. They may even, if the author is a visiting overseas VIP, announce the signing as a public event, so that queues trail in from the street as people line up to meet someone they have always wanted to meet.

For the most part, though, book signings are a mixture of cheery irrelevance and small sales. People visiting the shop decide they want to meet you, but not buy your book. Aspirant writers visiting the shop – and remember, by their nature, aspirant writers are attracted to bookshops – decide they want to meet you but not buy your book while getting advice from you on how to publish their own book. It is your job to engage with each and every one of them, be helpful where you can, but keep them moving so that the wonderful individual who arrives clutching three copies of your novel, with instructions as to precisely what they want you to write on each, gets the attention they deserve.

Some writers – inevitably, the best known and most acclaimed – can, and do subvert the book-signing process. One of them is John Banville, who told *The Irish Times*'s Fiona McCann that when he does book signings, he's filled with the desire to tell those who approach him: 'I'm not the person who wrote the book. The person who wrote the book ceased to exist every time I stood up from my desk. Somebody else wrote the book.' If Banville ever does tell this to book-buyers at a signing, the chances are that it will add to what he sees as, 'great disappointment on the part of the readers'.

'You can see them looking at you and saying, "God, he's a lot shorter than I expected."'

Bad enough to have bookshop customers deciding you're a bit on the short side. Much worse is the possibility of no bookshop customers at all. That's what every writer dreads; a signing when nobody visits the table and passersby elude the writer's eye as if a mutual glance would give them a bad case of the bends. If the bookshop is well organised, they will send an assistant over to have a brief chat with you, to interrupt the stretch of boredom and idleness. If they don't, you sign a few books to have them ready (because the bookshop can use them later, anyway, and may even stick a gold label on the front, declaiming 'Signed by the Author.') Smile at passers-by and look happy, even if you aren't. The staff in bookshops make decisions about authors, based on their behaviour at signings. If a writer is upbeat and amicable, staff members are much more likely to recommend the book to a customer who seeks a bit of advice before they purchase.

Writers and their publishers are in a marketing partnership, these days, which requires the writer to devote several weeks to the flogging of their latest book. Learn to like it and look as if you like it.

It may include a media tour.

The American media tour, as thriller writer William Caunitz sees it, is 'very hard, very demanding'. You will fly into a city, you will do five radio shows and maybe four press interviews and television shows, you go back to your hotel room, have a bite to eat, go to bed, get up in the morning and fly out again or perhaps fly out the same night to another city. That's what it's like and it's that way city after city. You get off the plane. You're met by an escort service with a car and they take you to all your appointments.

The trend towards an 'escort service' is in sharp contrast to the experience of Irish writers selling their wares in America a few decades back. At that stage, not only did publicists like Letty Cottin Pogrebin meet, greet and mind writers, they tried to keep Irish writers like Brendan Behan sober for the duration of the tour – with varying degrees of success.

The first time you do an author tour, you feel like a celebrity. Thereafter, it can become onerous, especially if – like Cathy Kelly – your work is hugely popular in Australia and New Zealand and you must take a week or ten days or longer away from your family.

'It's not good for marriages, it's not good for one's soul and it's not good for the work because it takes away a solid chunk of writing time,' was Evan Hunter's view.

On the other hand, in Ireland, the media tour is shorter and may involve no travel at all. The first target programme will be what it has always been, *The Late, Late Show*.

It has always been easier for book publicists to pitch a non-fiction title to that programme – indeed to most programmes – than a fiction title, because a novelist can't tell the story of their book without making viewers feel they don't need to buy it and nothing bores TV viewers quite as readily as artists talking about the making of their art, whereas a non-fiction book introduces new information or ideas or a new slant on existing information and ideas. TV programmes love the possibilities presented by a controversial programme which can give rise to a good studio digging match, so even a book about, say, why career women are happier if they don't have any children, is always likely to make it on to the programme because it's easy to find a panellist or other contributor to describe the author as unnatural, uncaring and basically a hard-faced bitch.

Because I've been training writers for national and international media appearances since TV programmes emerged from the primeval slime, you would expect me to say that writers who are trained do much better on media than untrained writers. So I'll say that. Writers, particularly of fiction, find it enormously challenging to shill for their *oeuvre*. Many of them meet a programme researcher and intimidate or bore them so that the researcher warns the presenter and producer against including the writer in a programme.

Some, having come through that process, then freeze up during the programme, thereby dropping the researcher in the mire ('You swore she'd have interesting stories to tell and would cry about her mother.') or are simply bland.

Every now and then, a writer survives a TV programme intact but completely forgets to remind viewers of the title of their book. American publicists demand (when they train Irish writers for American media) that authors become accustomed to giving the title of their book every forty-five seconds.

Naming the title of the book once in four minutes is too much for novice writers, who talk vaguely about 'my work,' 'the novel,' or, 'this latest book'. This makes the TV presenter happy, since it conveys the message that this is a real item as opposed to a free book plug, and makes the publisher commensurately unhappy, because viewers have no information on which to follow up any interest the writer may have conjured up in them.

Writers new to the publicity tour are often astonished to find that they don't necessarily get to meet the presenter of a major TV programme before they encounter them, live, on the air. They are even more discomfited by not being told, in advance, what the interviewer is going to ask them. The reverse is even more problematic: some TV programmes require the writer to deliver to the presenter, live on the air, precisely the same yarns in precisely the same order as they told the researcher.

One of the reasons for training in advance is because TV (although it should never have been invented and should be abolished because it delivers so little content, absorbs so much human time, contributes to obesity and anti-social behaviour and skews the world view of those who watch it a lot), is unnerving for newcomers. TV studios which, viewed on your home television set, seem to have the solidity of Everest, may not exist at all.

In the case of TV3, for example, the beautiful broken-up background to the *Midday* programme is a benign con perpetrated on viewers by technology. Colette Fitzpatrick and company sit in front of a big blank blue wall, onto which is projected the visuals which appear behind them in the transmitted programme, and woe betide someone who arrives in a blue dress, because the set will be projected on to that dress and their head will seem to be a free-floating entity, which is fine if they are publicising a sci-fi novel about headless Stepford wives, but a bit baffling otherwise.

If you go into the TV studio coasting on the comfortable conviction that, 'They'll ask me the right questions,' you are likely to come unstuck. This conviction may be based on the assumption that the interviewer will have read your book. Maybe, if you are being interviewed by a bookish bloke like Ryan Tubridy. Not guaranteed, in any other radio or TV studio. Accounts of book-ignorant interviewers happily insulting writers are legion. Ed McBain, who became the world's leading practitioner of police procedurals, got used to dealing with interviewers who had not read the latest – or any – of his books, but lost it when a radio presenter turned to him and said, 'I understand you've written a mystery?'

> I'd written a mystery? It sounded like I was a retired mailman who suddenly decided to write a mystery. I flared. I am sorry to say I flared and became somewhat immodest. I said, 'I am the pre-eminent mystery writer in the world.' I don't remember where the interview went from there.

Maeve Binchy, in a TV studio in Birmingham, was asked a preliminary question by a young male presenter, just as his show was about to go on the air.

'Have you always made your own furniture?' he enquired.

'No, I've actually never made any furniture,' Maeve responded.

'Oh, you're the other one,' he said equably. 'You're the one who wrote the big book.'

Just remember, when you do TV and radio interviews, that bigger and better than you have suffered on media in order to sell their books. That is the purpose. Take the pain. Remember, too, that TV notifies an audience about the publication of a book. Radio motivates them to go looking for it that day. So do not turn down the opportunity to do an interview with some small local radio station in Donegal. Several hundred committed readers may listen to that station, which may give you sufficient time to give those readers a riveting insight into your book and motivate them to go out after the programme and buy it.

Orange Prize winner Linda Grant has suggested that being young, camera friendly and media competent may, now, be a factor influencing publishers to look more favourably on manuscripts produced by such writers, and less favourably on those offered by older, less attractive writers. Grant wrote in *The Guardian:*

> To get the book into the hands of the reader requires marketing and publicity. Can you place an interview with a fifty-seven year old retired teacher in the pages of *Vogue*? No, you emphatically cannot. Can you place an interview with a twenty-five-year-old babe who has previously written a *zeitgeist* column for a Sunday newspaper? Yes, and not just in *Vogue* but virtually anywhere. Publishing has indeed become a beauty context. Good-looking people sell everything, everywhere, and books are no exception.

Scott Meredith, the literary agent whose company is now an international force (See Chapter 12), would have agreed with Grant up to a point. Meredith believed that 'some authors should never be seen'. On the other hand, the late Frank McCourt was neither young nor good looking when *Angela's Ashes* was published and publicised. He was charming on media, but his book made it onto the bestseller lists through word of mouth, rather than marketing. The same is true of Nuala O'Faolain's first book, *Are you Somebody?*, although an appearance on the *Late, Late Show*, then hosted by Gay Byrne, certainly helped.

Landing on the bestseller lists is not simply a function of publicity. When Maeve Binchy was told that her *Light a Penny Candle* was going to be a bestseller, she was astonished:

'I thought it was going to be like the book of short stories: that I would have to be down on my hands and knees rooting in the back of shops trying to drag it out to the front,' she remembers. Instead, when paperback houses started to bid for the rights as soon as the hardback came out, she was told that bestseller status was guaranteed.

She was also told that the paperback rights had been sold for the then phenomenal price of £52,000.

'Is that for you or for me?' she asked the hardback publisher.

'Two thirds of it is for you and one third of it is for me,' was the answer. Maeve thought the tone of the answer indicated a bit of envy on the publisher's part.

Budd Schulberg's first novel was a phenomenal bestseller called *What Makes Sammy Run?* (1941), about a character named Sammy Glick. It started as a series of short stories and might have stayed in that small market had it not been for an editor who read the stories and rang Schulberg to suggest that, unbeknownst to himself, he had the makings of a novel in them.

He told me some years ago: 'I would say becoming a bestseller first time out is not the healthiest thing for a writer because for one thing you're facing the second book, the burden of trying to meet the standards either artistically or commercially. Any second novel is enough of a challenge without that extra burden.'

Schulberg survived bestseller status. Not everybody does. The man who wrote the book on which the play (and film) *Mr Roberts* was based (originally published in 1946) was so overwhelmed by his initial success that he never wrote anything else of moment and died shortly afterwards, in 1949. As did Margaret Mitchell after the unprecedented sales and movie of *Gone with the Wind*.

None of which is to suggest that you should want to avoid the bestseller lists. Just that you put it in a wider context. Books by writers in the 1930s and 1940s like Sinclair Lewis, William Faulkner and John Steinbeck stayed on the shelves of the bookshops for much longer than would their equivalent today, and, in their case, sold a few thousand copies over several years, often losing money for their publisher in the process. Publishers were proud to have a William Faulkner on their list and they did not care if he sold only 2000 copies a year.

At the beginning of the 1940s, however, someone at the *New York Times* had the bright idea of publishing a weekly list of the books that had sold best in the previous week. The methodology of this definitive bestseller list is classified as a trade secret by the paper, but one of its organisers told me that it's 'essentially the number of books sold in general book stores, airport shops and regular commercial establishments around the country, gathered on the basis of a representative national sample of bookshops'.

From the outset, the very concept of a bestseller list was fraught with controversy, with publishers suggesting that a shop which inadvertently stocked up too heavily on a book that then hadn't sold would exaggerate the figures delivered to the newspaper in the belief that inclusion in the bestsellers would help even a stinker to start moving. More recently, when computerised sales figures took over from individually reported sales, such conspiracy theories faded somewhat, although in Ireland, some writers are convinced that if they send their friends repeatedly to some well-known bookshops to purchase their new book, it will end up on the lists of local bestsellers.

Landing on the *New York Times* bestseller list and staying there for even a few weeks (as opposed to the ten years achieved by some of the Harry Potter books) multiplies the earnings of the writer by an unbelievable quantum. Many purchasers of books buy only bestsellers, on the grounds, it can be assumed, that this guarantees the books won't be boring. Bookshops report people arriving in clutching the latest list and wanting to buy the new arrivals on it. Paperback publishers can then put a streak across the front of the book, describing it as a bestseller, and hardback publishers can put 'from the bestselling author of' or 'the latest bestseller from' on the front of the next offering from the same author. If the second book also makes it on to the bestseller lists, the writer is well on the way to becoming a brand, which will be reflected, over time, in the growth of the space given to their name on the cover of each emerging book, since this name is now the guarantee readers seek: the latest Faye Kellerman or Cathy Kelly or Gene Kerrigan.

This effect is further enhanced by the discounting policies of booksellers. Ten years ago, Amazon started to cut by 50 per cent the prices of books that appeared on the *New York Times* bestseller list, and now, that website runs its own lists of which books are doing particularly well, thus contributing to a marketing cycle which starts with the selection of a title, the design of a cover and – in the case of publishers outside Ireland – the allocation of an advertising budget.

Occasionally – very occasionally – a book becomes a bestseller by a circuitous route unrelated to marketing, and without any advertising spend, as happened to Rita Mae Brown's *Rubyfruit Jungle*. Rita Mae wrote the novel – still in print – when she was twenty-seven. It was one of the early ventures into what is now a separate genre – the gay novel. It was not warmly received by any of the big publishing houses she approached. She remembers:

> I had splinters in my nose from the best doors in town. I stood in their hallways and got the manuscript thrown back in my face. Everybody said, 'We don't like this book.' They either said, 'You're a pervert, die,' or they said, 'You can't write,' or just, 'Never darken our doors again.' I think I was too dumb to give up. Then an oil heiress opened a little teeny press called Daughters' Press. Her children were grown, so she decided to open up a feminist press in 1971 and she said, Here, I'll give you $1000. Lets see what happens. It sold 70,000 copies without one ad ever being run. Then Bantam Books – they're no slouch – thought, 'Well, gee, maybe there really is something to this.' So they bought it from Daughters and then after that it was relatively easy to get publishers to buy my books.

Some of the publicity Rita Mae later attracted, because she was, for a while, known to be Martina Navratilova's lover, was irritating to her rather than useful in selling books but she has managed to straddle a number of genres, over forty years of writing, and produce bestsellers in all of them.

Two final warnings about publicity. No, three:

1. Keep it to discrete chunks of your year and try to achieve profile but not over-exposure. If you ask me what constitutes over-exposure, I have to confess that I don't know. I just know it's one of those conditions like swine flu or pregnancy that you know for sure you have but never really believed would happen to you.

2. Don't believe or quote your own publicity. Be like John Banville. Think of the person who wrote the book as separate from yourself, and keep yourself realistic, humble and busy. Just keep the cuttings – they can be useful for down-the-line marketing purposes.

3. Get a good website. No, don't go to an expensive website designer. One of your pals has a son or daughter who is a computer geek who loves this kind of stuff. Do a deal with them, instead.

Now comes the piece of advice to which you will pay no attention: be wary, once you have published, of allowing your website to push you into becoming a service for other writers. Several of my (mostly women) writer friends spend an unconscionable amount of their time as a free support service for would-be writers, out of the goodness of their oversized hearts, and they need a foot in the arse for it. Or else they should pay a gatekeeper to prevent them from spending their valuable writing time on other people, because, as one of the most generous, Cathy Kelly, puts it, 'I hate letting people down. I hate saying no, and I will always do it. I am a big sponge.'

Novelist Kate Thompson is a living example of the gains to be made from friendship with kindly 'big sponges'. 'If I hit a rough patch then I can ring Cathy Kelly or Marian Keyes and they're always ready with a few words of encouragement and support,' she told the *Irish Independent*:

> I think my editor in the UK finds the amount of support among writers here to be a bit surprising. However, Marian and Cathy are both well-established writers who are very generous with their time and support. Deirdre Purcell was actually the first person I approached about writing and she was so helpful. She told me that the most important thing was to persevere, persevere and persevere some more.

It's all heartwarming, as well as surprising, this generosity of established writers to other, newer writers. But the truth is that if you reach out a helping hand to others, you can turn into a writerly version of Kali, that Indian god with all the arms, and end up feeling harassed and pressured by the needs of others, while your own publisher is getting shirty about late delivery. Maeve Binchy, many years ago, worked out her own formula of approach to this issue:

> I get asked sometimes a question which is a very hard one to say no to. People say, 'I wonder could

you do me a great favour – could you look at this manuscript for me?' Or 'My daughter has written a thing: could she show you a few pages of it?' And I'm really very tough about that. I just don't have the time for a start. I have a little handout letter now which I sent to people. It says, 'I am returning your manuscript to you unread for two reasons: first of all I am in competition with you and I must not be allowed to see your ideas. And the second one is that you must send it to somebody who has the power to publish it or reject it.'

12

Getting an Agent

The agent is a businessperson, a negotiator and a bargainer who sells the various rights to an author's work at the highest possible prices and at the most advantageous terms.

Paul Reynolds, Literary Agent

In the late 1870s, the very first literary agent, A.P. Watt, set up in London. Up to then, writers either sold their own work to publishers or had friends or relatives represent them. Some publishers welcomed the new profession. Some, like William Heinemann, did not, believing that agent got in the way of the close relationship publishers should have with their writers.

As time went on individuals set up agencies in the United States and publishers realised that they could save the cost of what where then called 'first reader departments', set up to discover new writers, if they let literary agents undertake the first trawl for them, free of charge. Some agents would claim that out of fifteen writers who seek their services, they accept one, although even this figure seems to me to be on the high side. And, according to Scott Meredith, a legendary American literary agent who established his own agency sixty years ago, acceptance can lead to a connection as intimate as a marital relationship. Meredith, who ran his agency until he was in his seventies, gave his home telephone number to all his clients and had no problem if they telephoned him in the middle of the night. His constant willingness to help writers extended to money:

> We loan money to authors all the time. We have a
> fund of around two million from which we advance
> money to authors. We will loan money to authors
> when they need money to continue a book or when
> they have to do some travelling.

Of course, by the time Meredith was lending his writers (including Norman Mailer) money, he could well afford it. By the 1990s, he owned a Rolls Royce, three other cars and what he described as 'a huge house', with a swimming pool and a tennis court. He could have retired, but still rose at five in the morning and worked as hard as he ever did, because, he said, as a literary agent, he never had a dull day. He loved battling with writers to get the best out of them and loved fighting on their behalf with publishers, to get the best for his clients out of them.

Most writers have the wrong idea about agents, seeing them as a combination of a high-powered sales representative and killer lawyer: knocking down doors, pulling in favours, persuading their existing contacts that they have, in this new writer, the ultimate stellar performer and beating a three-book deal out of them which runs into six figures, minimum. According to many of the established writers interviewed for this book, this is not the reality. They see agents as useful after you have already sold the first book. Few of them see agents as the hard-sell personal swat team of popular belief.

I've had a variety of experiences with agents. For most of my career, I worked without an agent. Then an American friend gave my book of short stories to David Mamet's agent, who took me on. Not much in the way of end results, because I think I landed in her books when she was coming to the end of her career, but such a charge to 'visit my agent in her office in Manhattan'.

Next, a cheque arrived for the German rights to one of my novels, together with a copy of the German edition. I wasted a bit of time going through the book to find out the German versions of the Dublin profanities with which the novel was loaded, then set out to find out how I had got lucky. It turned out that a man named John Spillane, the boss of Mercier Press, who'd brought out the novels, took them and other books to the Frankfurt Book Fair, talked civilly to overseas publishers, handed them copies of whichever book attracted them and filled up the resultant space in his luggage with contracts. It was not, of course, quite that simple, but this self-effacing quiet man was acting as my agent without being asked to, and remarkably successful he was at it, too.

Next, I wrote a book about plastic surgery, of which I've had a lot (and of which, if I could afford it, I'd have another lot, right this week). I wrote it without a publisher in mind, which, of course, is bad practice. Then, by accident, I had lunch with an old friend with whom I'd worked years ago in the Institute of Public Administration. Jonathan Williams, a big hirsute sparkly-eyed Welshman (yes, passionate about rugby, and yes, he does sing in a choir), thought the idea of the book was amusing and asked to see it. I sent it to him.

He read it and said he believed the best publisher for it was Lilliput Press. Anthony Farrell of Lilliput Press agreed and the outcome was *Mirror, Mirror: Confessions of a Plastic Surgery Addict*. Finally, I encountered a dauntingly athletic blonde named Tracy Brennan on a flight from the US which nearly ended in the Atlantic. Tracy's agency specialises in selling the work of Irish writers into the US and so far she's done remarkably well with one of my books.

Bottom line? I've never had a bad experience with an agent. Having one working on a book removes from me the fleeting notion that I should pay attention to the detail of any contract and none of them have made me rich. But then, I haven't made any of them rich, either, so that's a win/win.

I didn't discover until after he'd volunteered to take care of *Mirror, Mirror* that Jonathan Williams can't take on half the writers who want him to represent them. Even the Irish agents who have websites don't regard the websites as a means of advertising for writers. Anybody can get writers. It's successful writers everybody wants. Except, of course, that some successful writers believe they can manage just fine without an agent at all. Joseph Wambaugh, author of *The Choirboys*, refuses to work with an agent, believing that by saving the 15 per cent of his royalties he might otherwise have to shell out to an agent, he saves an enormous amount of money, out of which he pays a much smaller sum for a lawyer to look over any contract he is offered before putting his signature on it.

At the other end of the spectrum, some writers are approached by agents eager to work for them. Linda Grant, winner of the Orange Prize for *When I Lived in Modern Times*, was a well-established journalist when she was approached by a literary agent, who saw in her the potential to produce a book. Grant says that only through having contacts with media did she 'get round the problem of being over forty and not a babe when I published my first novel.'

If you want to have an agent, you contact the one you believe best suited to your kind of work, send them samples and if they agree, sit down and discuss how best to achieve what you, as a writer, want to achieve. Or get a reference from someone who is a friend of the agent you wish to connect with.

'The way things happen is by recommendation,' the *Irish Independent* quotes agent Marianne Gunn O'Connor as saying. 'We want to find new authors but everyone thinks they can write a book, that everyone has a story, that being a writer is utterly amazing, and you can earn millions of dollars.'

If you're looking for an agent in the US, make sure the one you contact is endorsed by the Association of Authors Representatives (AAR). They have a list of approved agents. One of the factors that distinguishes approved agents from others is whether or not they charge a fee for reading material. The general advice has always been that any agent who charges a fee to look at your manuscript should be avoided like swine flu, on the basis that an agent should earn their money by selling your work, not reading it.

However, this is one of the areas of change in the publishing business where the lines are less rigid than they used to be. Some of the larger agencies now have separate wings which do nothing but read manuscripts for a fee. Some of the smaller agencies have an up-front reader's report service listed on their website, which requires any author submitting a manuscript to pay them anything from $500 to

$5000 to read and report on the manuscript. It's a hell of a span, but don't rule out the $500 if it guarantees an expert's view of your manuscript and how you might improve it before it would be worth their while to represent you. Even $5000 may be a small price to pay, up-front, if it saves you months of toing and froing, at the end of which you have no sale and feel bitter and twisted towards the agent who took you on. Disappointed expectations are the bane of a writer's life. In relation to agents, as in relation to publishers, editors, producers and life generally, expect the worst and you will consistently be positively surprised.

13

Self-Publishing

The Reader
He is so stupid you can't trust him with an idea.
He is so clever he will catch you in the least error.
He will not buy short books.
He will not buy long books.
He is part moron, part genius and part ogre.
There is some doubt as to whether he can read.
John Steinbeck in a letter to his editor, Pascal Covici

It used to be called 'vanity publishing,' and provoked the same reaction as a whiff of the scent of the local landfill site. Nobody worthwhile would ever publish their own work. You mean pay out money to a printer to fill your garage with a volume no publisher would accept in order to have the dubious pleasure of handing copies of your unpublishable material to a few pals? The shame of it. Vanity publishing was regarded as pointless, because none of the bookshops would stock a book so published. It wouldn't sell, so what was the point?

Except that a few formidable writers were first self-published, including Mark Twain and Charles Dickens. Not to forget Norman Dacey. Norman who? Dacey. Not a household name this side of the Atlantic. Not – to be honest – a household name on the other side of the Atlantic, either. But remember what we said earlier about the richest writers in Ireland being anonymous lads producing school textbooks. Norman was the American parallel. He wrote a book entitled *How to Avoid Probate*. He failed to engage a publisher in it but decided that it should still be published, because he believed it had a market. So he ran off an initial private printing of 10,000. The size of that initial printing – in advance of the internet – is testament to his faith. That faith was justified, and when commercial publishers saw the numbers, they realised this was one not to pass up, and Norman went from self-publishing to being the offering of a standard publishing house.

If you have reached the stage where you're tired of trekking between rejections, then consider self-publishing. In Ireland, a self-publishing house named Trafford has an excellent website, offering straightforward deals ranging from economy to first class. Some 'sponsored' publishing houses claim to have editors on board who will improve your manuscript in much the same way as an orthodox publisher's editor would. If you decide to go with sponsored publishing and you land with a house that doesn't have this facility, find a freelance with experience in this area, remembering that a sponsored publishing house without an editor is little more than a printer. In fact, you might be better to get your book edited by a freelance editor and then printed.

A friend of mine named Ronnie Devlin has much experience in the communications area, having served as a press officer in a government department. He tried his hand at writing a novel and eventually published it himself. This is

Ronnie Devlin's first-person account of the experience, with all its joys and limitations.

Self-publishing – The Jimmies – *A First-Hand Account*
'If you are expecting a well-researched, in-depth, piece on self-publishing, please stop reading. Skip to the next section. Right now. However, if you seek a real-life self-publishing story, read on. This short account proves that it is not only possible but relatively easy to see your name on the spine of your very own book.

'Some time in 2003, I spotted a newspaper advertisement that promised a publishing contract for the best outline of a novel accompanied by the first chapter. This didn't really seem too much of a challenge. As a long-term, frustrated, would-be writer, I had one or two ideas floating around in my head.

'A couple of days later, I had finalised an outline and the first chapter of *Seventeen at Forty-Four* – a story of a man whose emotional development had not kept pace with his status in society or with his age. My beautiful concept was based on a number of not-so-carefully researched beliefs:

- The majority of successful Irish authors were female and, from a male perspective, that simply wasn't fair.
- Chicklit was taking over the world and it had to be stopped.
- Roddy Doyle didn't write funny, touching, books any more and I, and many of my friends, missed that genre.

'Nothing ever came back to me on foot of my submission. However, the fact that a first chapter was stored on the laptop served to encourage me to further develop the book.

'At the time, I had been doing a quite a bit of foreign travel – generally alone and arriving on foreign soil the evening before meetings. What was a fellow to do in such circumstances? Some early trips had brought me to the dreaded Irish pub. But on one visit, I turned first to the mini-bar in the hotel room, then to the laptop. And the story of Jimmy Moran, largely unplanned, began to take shape. For the next six to eight months, Jimmy was my travelling companion. He shared every hotel room I visited. And finally, in Geneva, he came of age. The book was completed.

'When I arrived home, I sent my manuscript to a well-known Irish publisher. I got my reply within a couple of weeks: 'Sorry, that's not the kind of book we do. Anyway, our plans are well made for next year's titles.' When I investigated the type of book they specialised in, however, I discovered that, for them, chick-lit was the only game in town. A bit of web-research on other publishers showed that my manuscript would not be long enough to be considered for commercial publication. I needed another twenty thousand words. So, I gave a copy of the manuscript to a small number of people, hoping for honest, initial, feedback. What I got back was generally positive and also exactly what I needed – suggestions about broadening and deepening the storyline. Doing this, however, proved easier said than done. The insertion of any additional material had ramifications throughout the story. A considerable amount of reworking was needed – but, in dribs and drabs, I got this work done. It was almost time to approach publishers and literary agents – but this time,

I would do it right – strictly in line with the submission guidelines published on their websites and in *The Writers' and Artists' Yearbook*.

'I sent the outline and the initial chapters of the, now renamed, novel, *The Jimmies*, to as many appropriate publishers and agents as I could find.

'More disappointment. The replies, though very kind and encouraging, could have been summarised as: 'Times are hard in the publishing world. We're not taking any new writers on. No market for that sort of stuff. Have you a track record? Do we know you?'

'The dream of seeing *The Jimmies* in print was dead.

'During an idle afternoon in the rainy summer of 2008, I went back and reread the manuscript. It still made me laugh. So what good was it there on my laptop, if no one else would ever read it? Why not self-publish? After all, if it was good enough for the first edition of *The Commitments*, would it not be good enough for *The Jimmies*? I looked at a number of options – most involved the author paying rather a large sum of money up-front to a publisher who would arrange conversion to camera-ready text and supply perhaps a hundred copies of the book. Some involved creation of a website for sales or advertisement on the publisher's website. Frankly, it all seemed too expensive.

'I then recalled Les, a man I had met in a medical waiting room some years previously, telling me about Lulu.com. He said he had used it to produce a limited number of copies of a book, mainly aimed at family and friends. He said it was simple and what was even more interesting, he said there was a minimal up-front cash outlay.

'Les was right. I checked out the Lulu website and within

an hour, I had uploaded the Word-based text (almost 80,000 words) of *The Jimmies* and it was converted into pdf format I then chose a cover from a selection of stock covers and inserted front and back cover text. Job done. I ordered a copy to proofread. The total cost was €14.60, including post and packing from the US.

'A week later, the proof arrived. Yes, it looked like a paperback book. It smelled like a paperback book. By God, it was a paperback book – and it had my name on the cover...

'The rest of the story is simple enough. When I had done some minor editing work on the proof (redo the Word document and again convert to pdf), I set a price (based on the production cost of the book plus a royalty for me), got an American ISBN number for free (a special offer) and elected, via the Lulu website, to sell it directly through Lulu (in hard and soft copy) and through Amazon, with previews on these sites and on Google Books.

'The bottom line, for aspiring authors, is that self-publishing works. But it has to be seen for what it really is. It is not about vanity, by the way. It's about turning dreams into reality. And the dream of writing is never really about the hope of making a fortune from the book. It's about bringing one's creativity, one's story, to a wider public.

'There are many variations on the methodology. Lulu and similar sites require no major up-front payment but the price per copy is high. Other self-publishing operations require substantial payments up-front but give the author a number of copies of the book as part of the package.

'Here are some pros and cons of the Lulu model:

Pros

- The up-front cost is the equivalent of only one copy of the proof (based on the page count) plus postage and packaging.
- It is a simple procedure for anyone who dabbles on the internet.
- There are simple tools for layout and cover design.
- There is quick turnaround from submission to delivery.

Cons

- No professional advice to the writer – what would an experienced editor have suggested?
- Print-on-demand is very expensive, in spite of quantity discounts.
- Ultimately it's up to the wrier to find markets for the book.
- People automatically ask, 'Which bookshops stock your work?'But, unless you have a contact in the trade, you are relying on internet sales.

Some Necessities

- Get someone you trust to proof your copy.
- Don't be afraid to get some advice on your manuscript.
- Believe in your product – if you can cast off your ego and still honestly enjoy your book, someone else will be likely to enjoy it also.

And Finally, Some Lessons for this Writer

- Ignore the excitement of getting your first book published – don't give it away too easily because every copy presented to someone for free costs you money.
- Every person who buys the book and enjoys it is likely to pass it on to a friend or two – the sales count always under-reflects the readership.
- In spite of many good reviews from friends and strangers alike, it's virtually impossible to get anyone to post a positive review on the internet.
- Self-publishing frees you from the accepted norms of the publishing world: your book can be as short or as long as you want it to be and it doesn't have to fit into a recognised genre. This is a lesson that I intend to heed in writing my next book.
- Finally, and most importantly, the achievement is in enabling others to read your work – it's absolutely not about making a fortune.'

(*The Jimmies* by Ronald Devlin is available for purchase in hard copy and download at www.lulu.com. It's available in hard copy at www.amazon.co.uk.)

14

Writing for the Spoken Word

Imagine yourself at a dinner table back in the United States, with a local editor, a banker, and a professor, talking over the coffee. You try to tell what it was like, while the maid's boyfriend, a truck driver, listens from the kitchen. Talk to be understood by the truck driver while not insulting the professor's intelligence.

Broadcaster Edward R. Murrow, briefing his European staff during the Second World War

Writerly writers hate to admit it, but an enormous amount of what is written is not consumed from the page or even from the screen of a computer, Kindle or iPad. It comes at us from radio and television or from stages or platforms. Many writers forget this sizeable market, and far too many writers, when it comes to their attention, fail to recognise that it has demands and requirements which are not the same as those posed by the printed word.

Even if what is required is a speech, a television script or a radio talk, when a writer sits down at a computer keyboard, what tends to emerge is written rather than spoken English.

That's largely the result of education. We are trained to take the written word seriously. We write essays in college which accustom us to its structures, rhythms and formalities, so that even though the spoken word is used for as much as 80 per cent of our communication every day, the written word is the definitive version of the language, as far as we're concerned.

In fact, the spoken word is important from the moment we're born. The written word comes later. Much later. It is – as many people suffering from functional illiteracy can testify – possible to get through an entire adult life without learning how to read. It's difficult. It's energy-sapping. But it can be done. The spoken word is the first essential of communication. (Ask any crying baby.) The written word is less pivotal but is perceived as infinitely more valuable, partly because the evidence of its existence lasts, whereas, up to the twentieth century, records of the spoken word didn't. The lexicon of the written word is richer and its products last longer – hence Oscar Wilde's expressed regret that he had poured out his genius at dinner and lunch tables, rather than making sure his every *bon mot* was committed to print.

The written word is the equivalent of a motorway: barred to bikes, invalid carriages, learner drivers, animals and pedestrians. It requires a bit of training and effort and adults do most of it. The spoken word, on the other hand, is for all of us.

That's not to say that the spoken word cannot provide challenges. Ava Gardner memorably remarked of fellow film star Clark Gable that he was, 'the sort of man who, if you said, "Hello, Clark, how are you?" he'd be kinda stuck for an answer.'

Without being consciously aware of the difference between the spoken and written words, most of us instinctively make the necessary shifts. We speak in short sentences. We write in long sentences with subordinate clauses. We speak for immediate comprehension. We write for eventual comprehension. We speak with much more than words. We write with words alone and often too many of them. Take a look at the following two paragraphs. They're in the written word. But they're a written-word version of a story you're familiar with. Trust me, you are familiar with this story. See if you can identify it.

> The circumstances surrounding the individual at the nub of the issue would suggest a precipitate loss of disposable income, although this precipitate loss is unexplained and is juxtaposed against radically different social conditions affecting near although not blood relatives. It is clear, however, that an element of envy over relative pulchritude may have been instrumental in the absence of the normal female affiliation one might have expected between the two siblings and their adoptive family member.
>
> The crucial intervention of a third party resulted from a social engagement involving the siblings but specifically excluding the central figure who was on her own as a consequence of their departure when visited by an individual claiming a spiritual relationship with her. This visitor then caused the manifestation and mutation of rodents and vegetables into means of transport into which she embarked having first undergone significant alteration of raiment,

the latter involving items for the termination
of her nether limbs of doubtful durability but
immediate transparency.

That's the story of Cinderella with the written word
inflicted on it. In the spoken word, the teller says, 'Once upon
a time, there was a poor little orphan named Cinderella. She
lived with her stepmother and her two ugly sisters. They hated
her because she was so beautiful.'

Saying that 'an element of envy over relative pulchritude'
may have caused the problem wouldn't cut it with a four-
year-old. But moving into that kind of language, using what
Macauley called the 'big, grey words of the lexicon' doesn't
make it any better for anybody – of any age.

While not many people, asked to write down the story
of Cinderella, would go quite as far into the written word as
my example, the reality is that obscure writing is sometimes
regarded as good writing. It often looks impressive. Indeed,
most of us don't like the look of the spoken word when we see
it on a computer screen or on paper.

Nicholas George, a one-time Director of News for the
BBC, summed this problem up beautifully in a briefing
document for his reporters. He told them:

> The best radio writing usually looks unbeautiful in
> print. We're not used to it. We speak one way and
> write another. What we would like you to do is write
> the way most people speak. Most people speak in
> short sentences or half-sentences. The language is
> usually uncomplicated. When you write a radio
> report, the language has to be uncomplicated. The

language must be plain. Sentence structure should
be simple. Simple subject, simple predicate. No
compound sentences.

Bottom line: whether you're writing a speech or a radio
script or anything else for the spoken word, write it in the
spoken word and don't obsess over how oddly it looks in
print.

Speechwriters may choose, if a copy of the speech has to be
distributed to media or to the audience (always, please, after
the speaker has actually delivered it), to rewrite sections of it
so that it has longer sentences and looks more respectable. As
long as there is no significant difference between the spoken
word and the written word versions, this is acceptable. But, in
preparing the version your speaker will actually use, prepare
yourself and them for the fact that it won't look like a report.

It will, for example, have short sentences. Very short
sentences. Sentences that may have no verb in them. Sentences
beginning with 'And...' even if it would make the teacher who
taught you English apoplectic. Short sentences are easier to
read. Easier to hoover up off the page in one cognitive chunk
which can be delivered in toto to the audience before the
speaker goes back to the page for the next chunk. (It should
be made clear, here, that this is not the ideal way to deliver
a speech. However, many public figures find themselves
delivering more speeches in any given week than they could
hope to reduce to cards carrying trigger words, so whoever
writes their speeches must make those speeches easy to read
aloud.)

The rationale behind short sentences has been elaborated
in what's called the Fog Index, which does complicated

mathematics to illustrate that a sentence of fewer than eight words is easy to understand and that, as you double or treble the word count in any one sentence, the fog thickens around it, making it progressively more difficult to access its meaning at first hearing. When you've finished the first draft of something you intend to read aloud or have someone else read aloud, you can tell your computer to check for the length of sentences and cut the stalks down.

Another key characteristic of the spoken language is its use of first-degree words. A first degree word is one which instantly evokes a mental picture of what it means. 'Book,' 'boat' and 'cup' are examples of first-degree words.

Second-degree words almost have to be run through the first-degree filter before you know for sure what is being talked about. 'Volume,' for instance, can be used to describe a book, but it can also be a measure of quantity. It's a second-degree word. Similarly, 'vessel' or 'barque' are second-degree words for 'boat'. They're best used in the written word to avoid repetition, but in the spoken word, it's usually more helpful to the understanding of the audience if you stick with 'boat'.

When writing a speech, for yourself or anybody else, write as people actually speak, not as they should speak. Don't put words in a script you wouldn't use to one other human being across a desk or a table or in a pub. Never set out to impress – just to inform.

Make sure the words you give a speaker are words they can pronounce. Let's say your speaker is not adept with the sounds created by putting the tongue against the front teeth. So, instead of saying 'youth' they always say '*yout*'. It's your job, as their speechwriter, to substitute 'young people' for 'youth' wherever it happens in the speech. And never overestimate the knowledge of your speaker. Put in a phrase like 'an old adage' and sure as shootin', your speaker will mispronounce 'adage' to rhyme with the Frenchified pronunciation of 'garage' so they say 'the old adahghe' when they should be saying 'addidge'.

The best way to avoid this is to listen to the speaker reading the speech and take out anything that they stumble over. Insist on its removal. I once had a speaker who couldn't pronounce 'ethnic'. Every time he came across it in the speech, he said 'enthic'. I wanted to take it out. He wouldn't let me. He was convinced he could learn it and would be more impressive if he did. I yielded. I shouldn't have.

On the day, as the keynote speaker at a prestigious conference, he got through all of the 'ethnics' fine, but ended the speech by announcing he was going to leave the audience with a quotation from 'Oscar Wilde's *The Ballad of Reading* Goal.' If you have to include a challenging word, type it phonetically in the version the speaker plans to use. Not in the version that's going to be handed out to the audience or to journalists.

Active verbs improve written and spoken communication alike. It's simply better to say: 'The Volunteers occupied the GPO,' than it is to say: 'The GPO was occupied by the Volunteers.'

State, then qualify, is a vital rule in the spoken word. Consider this: 'There are exceptions to every rule, of course, and the metabolism of each individual is specific to them, which makes generalisations dodgy, but that said, it's fair to point out that a diet of chips and burgers makes people fat.'

By the time you have reached the last line of it, you've lost the will to live. And that's when it's in the written word in front of you. Say it as part of a speech or a script and your listeners will be totally confused by the time they get to the conclusion. You have provided them with too many distractions. Do it the other way around: 'A diet of chips and burgers makes people fat. Now, there are exceptions...' The initial statement establishes the issue. The modifications may be necessary in order that you be statistically accurate or for legal reasons, but they should come after the main statement, not before.

Mention people when it's natural is a rule of speechwriting that's easily forgotten, because we're so used, particularly when it comes to speeches, to a structure which puts thanks at the end, so that everybody from the plumber to the gravedigger receives gobs of gratitude in a wearying sequence. Much better to praise the plumber when you're telling the story of the burst pipe.

Postponement is impossible in the spoken word. Every time a speaker says, 'But I don't want to address that now,' or, 'More anon,' they create a distraction. This is made worse by leakage from the spoken word. The speaker who says, 'More on this following,' is as bad as the speaker who says, 'As I said above.' Above where?

The spoken word is *inclusive*. Inclusive means a lot more than using 'we' rather than 'I' or 'you' all the time. Franklin D. Roosevelt was once handed a speech in the middle of which was the line: 'We will strive to create an inclusive society.'

He opened his fountain pen and crossed out the line, substituting this one: 'We will build a society where nobody feels left out.' Roosevelt's substitution turned the sentence into inclusive English. Use enough inclusive language in a speech, and the audience transforms itself. It becomes the embodiment of the ultimate inclusive sentence, Shakespeare's 'We few, we happy few, we band of brothers...'

In the spoken word, *you never reverse to the point*. In the written word, this often happens. Take the written-word version of 'Cinderella' in this chapter.

> The crucial intervention of a third party resulted from a social engagement involving the siblings but specifically excluding the central figure who was on her own as a consequence of their departure when visited by an individual claiming a spiritual relationship with her.

In the spoken word, we cut to the chase. The fairy godmother appeared when poor Cinders was all on her own, crying because she couldn't go to the ball the ugly sisters had gone to.

Although the spoken word has many virtues, it develops its own brand of clichés. On radio, every day, you'll hear people make announcements like this: 'Later in the programme, we'll be looking at sex, lies and videotape. But first...'

'But first' is one of the maddeningly frequent clichés afflicting people who make their living behind a microphone. Speechmakers have their own clichés, starting with the lie about being delighted to be here today. Every speechwriter, in addition to a *Dictionary of Quotations* (to be sparingly used) should have a *Dictionary of Clichés* on their desk.

In the spoken word, *repetition is valuable*, where it allows the speaker to present a layered concept that increases in ferocity and meaning with every repetition. The great master-orator, when it came to the use of this device, was Churchill. On 4 June 1940, he made a speech, one paragraph of which is filed under 'half-remembered' in many heads:

We shall go on to the end, we shall fight in France, we shall fight on the seas and oceans, we shall fight with growing confidence and growing strength in the air, we shall defend our Island, whatever the cost may be, we shall fight on the beaches, we shall fight on the landing grounds, we shall fight in the fields and in the streets, we shall fight in the hills; we shall never surrender.

The repetition became like the beat of a war-drum – Churchill often used repetition, and often in threes. He also used sensational words – words that appeal to the senses – an essential of the spoken word. Remember 'Blood, tears, toil and sweat'? Each one of them talked to the senses of the audience. Anybody writing a speech should seek to make the listeners' sense of smell, touch, taste and hearing activate their imaginations. Great art is always a dialogue, not a statement, and a speech can be great art when it evokes real emotional response from listeners by making their senses come alive.

One of the devices of the spoken word which should be economically used is the rhetorical question. The rhetorical question is a question that doesn't expect an answer. In Sean O'Casey's *Juno and the Paycock*, one of the characters, Captain Boyle, is given to rhetorical questions.

'What is the stars, Joxer?' he asks his drinking buddy, knowing he'll sound philosophical and get no answer. 'What is the stars?'

On rare occasions, the rhetorical question can be useful, as it was in Churchill's first speech as Prime Minister of Great Britain during the Second World War, when he asked rhetorical questions and answered them himself:

> You ask, what is our policy? I can say: It is to
> wage war, by sea, land and air, with all our might
> and with all the strength that God can give us;
> to wage war against a monstrous tyranny, never
> surpassed in the dark, lamentable catalogue of
> human crime. That is our policy.
>
> You ask, what is our aim?
>
> I can answer in one word: It is victory, victory
> at all costs, victory in spite of all terror, victory,
> however long and hard the road may be; for
> without victory, there is no survival.

Unfortunately, the rhetorical question is often the lazy speechwriter's method of moving from one idea to the next:

- So why does this matter?
- What is the next step?
- What is the problem?
- Where do we go from here?

The safest rule to apply to the rhetorical question is to limit its use to one outing and one outing only per speech.

Have the Courage of Your Contractions
In the written word, we are formal, opting for the full words rather than contractions. When we speaking, though, we litter our sentences with 'didn't', 'couldn't' and other contractions. If you're writing for speech, write the way speech writes itself on the air: with lots of contractions.

Make Your Sums Add Up

Every now and then, you'll hear a traffic manager or an environmentalist on radio, bemoaning the fact that only 1.2 people travel in each car commuting into our cities each morning. It's a truly ridiculous image – and, remember, humans always produce mental images of what interests them. What's point two of a person? Head and shoulders? Torso?

Figures should always be given in terms which make them understandable at first hearing. (And don't evoke pictures of sawn-off commuter chunks in cars.) Reduce them to the simplest form you can. Three in every ten, rather than thirty one per cent. And don't put them in a list. If you give one set of figures, the audience will absorb them. Add a second and they stay with you. Add a third – and the earlier figures disappear out of their mental screen.

Do a Which Hunt

When you have your first draft complete, do a 'which' hunt. Tell your computer to find the word 'which' wherever it appears in the text. Then remove it. Its removal will make the speech more natural, not least because it commonly links two sentences that will be better, and briefer, on their own. But also because 'which' reeks of the written word.

Once the which hunt is complete, do padding removal. Here are some typical examples of things you should change:

- 'Factual information' *to* 'facts'
- 'At the present time' *to* 'now'
- 'In the event of' *to* 'If'

- 'A satisfactory consensus was reached.' *to* 'We agreed.'
- 'Incapacitated in the performance of her duties.' *to* 'Too sick to work.'

Timing

The final technical task for the speechwriter is timing. On average, 120 words take a minute to say. So if you're writing a ten-minute speech, 1,200 words will do it. However, if you're writing a forty-minute speech, don't produce 4,800 words. Keep it below four thousand words. When speechwriting, always underwrite. Nobody has ever complained about someone ending a speech five minutes early, and conference organisers love the early finisher, because it allows the conference to get back on schedule, having been knocked off it by the majority of speakers who grossly over-run.

TEN TIPS FOR SPEECH LAYOUT

1. Don't type it in capital letters. Capital letters are much more difficult to read than the usual mix of upper and lower case. We're used to the latter. Not used to the former.
2. Do use a serif typeface. A serif typeface is one like Minion (used here), where letters like M and N have little flat feet at the end of their uprights. A sans serif face is one like Arial, in which the letters don't have those feet. Serifs pull the eye forward and are easier for the speaker to read.
3. Do use big type. Big type is fourteen or sixteen point. Unless your speaker is legally blind, he or she is not

going to need anything larger than sixteen point. Indeed, if you go larger, so little appears on each page that a) the speech becomes disjointed and b) has so many pages that the audience think they're going to be stuck there until hell freezes over.

4. Do use big margins and double gaps between paragraphs. This lets the speaker add hand-written ideas. It also means that when they glance down, they can see where they are and what's coming up next.

5. Don't carry a sentence from one page to another. It's much easier for the person reading a speech if the sentence finishes on one page and a new idea begins on the next page. Making the transition from page to page while trying to finish a sentence throws most readers. Some speakers like to have the first three words that are going to appear on the next page put in the extreme right hand corner of the page they're reading. If that's what your speaker wants, give it to them.

6. Don't put instructions to the speaker in the text. Under pressure, they may read them out.

7. Don't staple the pages together. The speaker ought to be able to discard each page as it's read. In fact, speakers should always discard pages once they're done with them. Putting them at the back of the speech carries two dangers. The first is that the audience develops a hopeless conviction that this oration is going to go on for ever. The second is that the speaker may slide the page into the wrong place and encounter a page they've already read.

8. Do use thick paper. It's easier to hold and discard.

Thin paper, on the other hand, allows the reader to be distracted by the shadow-images of upcoming points.

9. Don't economise on paper. Finish an idea on one page, even if it leaves a gap. The gap is a cue to the reader that they need to pause before attacking a new theme on the next page.

10. Do paginate and order the pages. Every now and then, you get a speaker who is so challenged (never mind why) that, if page 9 is duplicated, they will read the same page all over again. Even worse is the situation where the speaker hasn't had a chance to check the script beforehand and discovers, on the podium, that page 9 is missing or blank. Double-check that the pages are numbered and in the right order. In the main script and in the reserve copy.

15

Writing a Blog

First, I'd become an avid reader of blogs, especially music blogs, and they seemed to be where the critical-thinking action was at, to have the kind of energy that I associate with rock writing of the 1970s or internet e-mail discussion lists a decade ago.

Carl Wilson

Melanie Morris earns her living with words. Her own and other people's. As editor of *Image* magazine, she selects, encourages, edits and publishes writers who produce features, profiles and snippets. As a columnist for the *Evening Herald*, she uses her own words and her own opinions to address whatever she fancies on any given week.

One of Melanie's *Herald* columns recently recorded the fact that a friend has been nagging her to start a blog. 'But at risk of upsetting and offending a whole "community" out there,' Melanie wrote, 'I hate the idea. I don't see the point and, more than that, I can't be bothered.'

As far as the *Image* editor is concerned, blogging is not far from keeping an electronic scrapbook, except that, in the case of a blog, the writer puts online whatever they've been doing or are thinking about, and finds the exercise enjoyable.

'Why should I do something for "fun", when it's my job to do it for money?' Melanie asked, mystified. 'Wouldn't that be like a surgeon spending a Sunday operating on his own leg for a bit of craic? Bloggers are basically the buskers of the internet. They come online, all self-important and opinionated, grab a pitch and start shouting loudly...Bloggers are wannabes with broadband...'

Ms Morris adds that for every Perez Hilton – the blogger who gained access to showbiz circles and became Lady Gaga's GBF (Gay Best Friend) – thousands of unknown bloggers are out there, reaching no more than a handful of readers and earning no money at it.

What she doesn't say is that journalism has become an oddity: the one profession whose members compete with themselves for free. As Nick Davies pointed out in *Flat Earth News*:

> ...some journalists write blogs without earning anything from it, their urge for self-expression obscuring from them the erosion of their own employing bodies represented therein. Why should readers buy newspapers when they can get the same writers on the Net at the drop of a keystroke?

When I echoed this point in the *Sunday Times* in 2009, I infuriated Adrian Weckler, who edits the consumer technology sections of the *Sunday Business Post* and keeps Matt Cooper of Today FM straight on the same topic. Adrian's view is that, while rich old traditional hacks may not want to have anything to do with blogging, 'a modestly paid young journalist, on the other hand, has little to lose by blogging.'

Little to lose – and perhaps something to gain. Blogging has been a showcase for some bloggers, who have ended up as columnists in newspapers or as proud owners of a contract to produce a book. They lay out their wares without charge online, a little like the delicious samples displayed at the end of a supermarket aisle at the weekend, in the hope that someone will decide to purchase them. A blogger who can prove themselves a prescient commentator or a smart wordsmith may attract the attention of an editor or a publisher or a programme maker. 'Blogging can be a key step to establishing somebody as a commentator, so they can do TV appearances and write a bestselling book,' says my Communications Clinic colleague, Gerard Kenny. 'Odd, but they are moving from new media to old – or at least straddling the two.'

One of Ireland's most successful bloggers, Suzy Byrne, has chosen to go from old media to new. While her current day job is as an advocate for people with disabilities, her past includes a book co-written at the age of twenty-three (*Coming Out*, with Junior Larkin, 1994), and a stint as columnist with *The Big Issue* and *Gay Community News*. In 2004, she became aware of a community of people publishing their ideas, bits of news, reactions and questions as blogs, and found the space intriguing:

> I'm a politics and news junkie, and have been since I was ten years old. I'd watch TV news all day if I could. But I don't want to be a journalist. I just love the fact that a young mother living in the arsehole of nowhere can go online and write stuff and

> engage with other people. I love the fact that we
> watch television in a quite new way: with a laptop
> on our knee, ready to react, ready to engage.

The fact that the blogosphere can't be controlled – a huge worry to other people – is one of the factors attracting Suzy, who sees it as an instantaneous free conversation between citizens who, because they don't have a big name, are not likely to have their opinions published in newspapers and magazines. When she won two major awards as a blogger (her site is mamanpoulet.com) she was slightly disappointed, because there hadn't been more competition for the awards.

Although she occasionally does features for newspapers and admires Sarah Carey, who started as a blogger and is now a columnist with *The Irish Times*, that's not where she wants to be. Nor does she want to be a guru, giving talks about how to blog. The free exchange of ideas is what fascinates her. She is amused at the way people suspicious of this space worry about its ethics, although she admits she's bothered when she reads about American or British political advisers coming to Ireland to teach local politicians how to blog and even more bothered by the new phenomenon of politicians hiring other people to blog on their behalf, under their name. 'Paying someone to blog for you I don't like. That's a whole different tone.'

It costs Suzy Byrne less than €100 a year to maintain her blog site and she'd be happy to do it for free simply to be part of what she calls 'the conversation', neither earning a fee nor seeking advertising. A precedent for this kind of sharing was set by computer heads who for some time have been writing software and giving it away for nothing. Their motives are interesting and mixed. Some wish to be of public service. Some have a marginally more subversive agenda, like the software engineers who developed OpenOffice to provide a free alternative to the global giant Microsoft.

One of the problems with blogging is that it's not always easy to work out if there's a hidden commercial motive behind a blog. In *The Cult of the Amateur,* Andrew Keen pointed to a new trend:

> Blogs are increasingly becoming the battlefield on which public relations spin doctors are waging their propaganda war. In 2005, before launching a major investment, General Electric executives met with environmental bloggers to woo them over the greenness of a new energy-efficient technology.

The problem, of course, is that bloggers may not be honest about their commercial affiliations – they may hide the fact that their views are bought and paid for by a commercial entity and that their blog, in consequence, is a dishonest vehicle for covert corporate propaganda. In the US, some of those involved in this kind of illegitimate spin haven't even bothered to cover their tracks. One blogger who wrote about the wonders of Wal-Mart turned out to be echoing, word for word, press releases turned out by the corporation's PR company.

While some PR companies are prepared to use blogs in this way, most reject it and, as a result, are infuriated when reporters ring them up asking for comment on behalf of one of their clients on a statement made in some blog. For a busy PR executive, having to cope with unchecked and uncontrolled allegations made by someone who may or may not have the evidence to support them is an unreasonable imposition, made more infuriating by the fact that the reporter following up this 'lead' may shruggingly admit that it is without legitimacy, but, like Everest, it's there.

Adrian Weckler's writings clearly establish that he doesn't like this kind of use of blogging, although he does suggest that it mightn't be a bad idea for PR people to sit down with and get to know prominent bloggers who inform public thought through their postings. He has no problem with overt commercial bloggin: 'Many blogs are company/work hybrids,' he notes. 'Beaut.ie is a very successful blog. But it is a company now, really. They are pretty commercial now. There are a couple of cycling blogs that would fall into the same category.'

If we take the term 'bloggers' as referring to people who are not overtly posting company stuff but who engage in commentary (and maybe some reporting) on a regular basis, Weckler suggests that while bloggers may form a community, it isn't a rich community:

> Of these people, very few make money directly from their blogging activities. I'd say it is certainly under 10 per cent. Mick Fealty (Slugger O'Toole) signed a deal with *The Guardian/The Observer* over a year ago, to use material from his blog. Niall Byrne (www.nialler9.com) attracts significant advertising interest to his site, as his is one of the biggest of the Irish blogs, attracting several thousand visitors every day.

Some smaller blogs attract Google ads but the advertising spend is not sizeable in Ireland. Suzy Byrne reckons that if she was in America, her blog could make her a lot of money, as could those of several other writers, whereas the Irish market isn't big enough to make anybody rich. This doesn't matter, if you are not primarily motivated by money.

Many bloggers connect with the wider world through their blogs. They don't need or want to go to nightclubs, receptions or press conferences. They don't need or want to dress up and be known in person. Having their views, insights or news picked up on and reacted to is what they want. Bloggers sharing a point of view often find themselves within a spontaneously-erupting cluster of like-minded people, which is arguably as rewarding as if not more rewarding than a better-paid staff job in some newspapers. It's a whole new series of choices for writers:

1. Publish a blog without wanting to be paid – simply, like Suzy Byrne, to share ideas, news and a sense of community.
2. Publish a blog in the hope of attracting enough regular visitors to justify someone investing advertising money in it.
3. Publish a blog as a marketing device for your writing – blogging in the hope of attracting an agent, a publisher, a radio or TV producer or an editor locked into 'old media' who might hire you.
4. Publish a blog as an adjunct to the day job.
5. Publish a blog as a way of keeping alive the relationship with those who read you in 'old media'.

Number 4 is a growing sector. Many newspapers now carry blogs by their correspondents on the newspaper website. This allows political correspondents to react faster to emerging news than the printed paper allows. It also allows them to publish material for which their print editor couldn't find space – a particular problem of the past few years of downturn, when newspapers slimmed down to skeletal thinness as a result of lack of advertising. Some correspondents who wouldn't have been seen dead in the blogosphere four years ago are now regular bloggers. Some of them shrug and enjoy it. Some of them shrug and decidedly don't enjoy it, feeling either that they're being forced to do twice as much work for half the money (join the majority, lads), that having to produce so many words so quickly may diminish the quality of their output, or that material going on to a blog site is not subject to as many checks and balances as if it were destined for print media.

Increasingly, writers of books are maintaining blogs as a way of keeping connected with readers of those books. (Or, in some cases, not keeping connected with those readers: novelist Marian Keyes, in the depths of depression in 2009, sent the message to frequent visitors to her site that, since she was too ill to write or read or eat, she was also unable to put messages up on her blog site.) Publishers like writers to maintain blogs because it reminds journalists about their presence and alerts readers to upcoming titles.

This does, however, have a downside. The wonderful comfort of blogging into a space occupied by people who already like you beats writing the next chapter of a book, hands down, and the strange under-researched fact is that nobody ever developed writer's block as a blogger, maybe because plotting, developing character and writing conversations that sound as if they were uttered by real people is one hell of a lot more difficult than recounting yesterday's domestic hassle or the plans for next week's anniversary.

The sense of community provided by blogging, both negative and positive, should never be underestimated. Some bloggers overseas, including big names, have stopped blogging because they found the random venom of response too daunting. When bloggers are nasty, they're very, very nasty and they have no editor to control them.

On the other hand, when bloggers are pleasant, they're very, very pleasant. They will go out of their way to speedily supply a bit of information or a link that might be helpful. When this happens to a blogger, it creates an astonishing sense of connectedness – and this sense of connectedness can be two-way, which in turn points to increasing use of blogs (not to mention Twitter) as a political force.

'There are some people blogging away at the moment who will be using this, instead of working for the local party machine, as the first step in a political career,' Gerard Kenny, who has worked with countless aspirant and successful politicians, maintains. 'If you are able to point to a couple of thousand people from Waterford regularly visiting your blog, it might be a persuasive argument for a party picking you to run – although this is probably a decade away.'

Maybe. Or maybe not. According to Ivan Yates, former Fine Gael minister, owner of Celtic Bookmakers and ubiquitous old-media practitioner, 'The campaign dialogue of the future will be databases, incessant emails and blogs – goodbye door knocking.'

I was forced to cave in on the blogging front by my editor,

who insists I blog each week on the Londubh site about ways of saving time. Melanie Morris, editor of *Image*, is likely to hold out longer than I did.

'I think you can safely assume that I won't be starting a blog any time soon,' she says. 'And as for all you shouting away in the blogosphere out there, didn't anyone ever suggest a diary?'

BIBLIOGRAPHY

Bauby, Jean-Dominique. *The Diving Bell and the Butterfly*. London: Vintage, 1996.

Block, Laurence. *Telling Lies for Fun and Profit: A Manual for Fiction Writers*. New York: William Morrow, 1981.

Brande, Dorothea. *Becoming a Writer*. Foreword by Malcolm Bradbury. London: Pan Books, 1996.

Brown, Rita Mae. *Starting from Scratch*. New York: Bantam, 1989.

Buckley, William F., Jr. *Miles Gone By*. Washington: Regnery, 2004.

Dash, Mike. *Satan's Circus: Murder, Vice, Police Corruption and New York's Trial of the Century*. London: Granta, 2008.

Davies, Nick. *Flat Earth News: An Award-winning Reporter Exposes Falsehood, Distortion and Propaganda in the Global Media*. London: Chatto and Windus, 2008.

Derber, Charles, William A. Schwartz and Yale Magrass. *Power in the Highest Degree*. Oxford: Oxford University Press, 1990.

Gardner, John. *On Becoming a Novelist*. New York: W.W. Norton and Company, 1999.

Goodwin, Kearns, Doris. *Team Of Rivals: The Political Genius of Abraham Lincoln*. New York: Simon and Schuster, 2006.

Keen, Andrew. *The Cult of the Amateur: How Blogs, MySpace, YouTube and the Rest of Today's User-Generated Media are Killing our Culture and Economy.* London: Nicholas Brealey, 2008.

King, Stephen. *On Writing.* New York: Scribner, 2000.

Lane, Christopher. *Shyness.* Connecticut: Yale University Press, 2007.

McCarthy, Ava. *The Insider.* London: Harper Collins, 2009.

McCollister, John. *Writing for Dollars: 75 Tips for the Freelance Writer.* New York: Barnes and Noble, 1995.

Nolan, Liam (with John Nolan). *Secret Victor: Ireland & the War at Sea 1914-1918.* Cork: Mercier Press, 2008.

Purcell, Deirdre. *Diamonds and Holes in My Shoes.* Dublin: Hodder Headline Ireland, 2006.

Raabe, Tom. *Biblioholism.* Toronto: Fulcrum Publishing, 1999.

Steinbeck, John. *Journal of a Novel: The East of Eden Letters.* New York: The Viking Press, 1969.

Todorov, Tzvetan. *Facing the Extreme, Moral Life in the Concentration Camps.* New York: Metropolitan Books, 1996.

Wright, Thomas. *Oscar's Books.* London: Chatto and Windus, 2008.